COOPERATIVES A

COOPERATIVES AND AGRIBUSINESS

By

Dr. S. Nakkiran
Professor
Department of Cooperatives
Institute of Cooperatives & Development Studies
Ambo University, Ambo
Ethiopia
Mail: doctorsnakkiran@gmail.com

&

Dr. M. Karthikeyan
Assistant Professor
Department of Cooperatives
Faculty of Business & Economics
Hawassa University
Hawassa
Email: mkeya2003@gmail.com
mkeya2003@yahoo.com

DPH

DISCOVERY PUBLISHING HOUSE PVT. LTD.
NEW DELHI-110 002

Published by:
Tilak Wasan
DISCOVERY PUBLISHING HOUSE PVT. LTD.
4383/4A, Ansari Road, Darya Ganj
New Delhi-110 002 (India)
Phone : +91-11-23279245, 43596064-65
Fax : +91-11-23253475
E-mail : parul.wasan@gmail.com
discoverypublishinghouse@gmail.com
web : www.discoverypublishinggroup.com

***First Edition:* 2012**
ISBN: 978-93-5056-071-6

Cooperatives and Agribusiness

Printed at:
Shree Balaji Art Press
Delhi

Preface

Agribusiness is one of the emerging academic areas that is gaining currency. Almost all universities have started introducing this course in various disciplines like agricultural economies, economics, rural development, cooperation, resource management etc. This course is typical in itself, in the sense it has more application than theoretical oriented. This is a marked different subject, compared to other courses of study. We have made good attempt to shape this book and frame lessons to suit the needs of the academic requirements. This book is divided into Eight Chapters. The Chapter 1 deals with the Rural Economy of Ethiopia and the relevance of agribusiness. Chapter 2 deals with the constraints in agribusiness. Here we have given an account of nature of demand and supply of agricultural commodities. Chapter 3 is about the infrastructure needed for agribusiness. Infrastructures like transport, communication and warehousing that are needed for this business are dealt in detail. In Chapter 4, the socio-cultural factors that decide the opportunities for agribusiness are explained. Opportunities in agribusiness and how to utilize the resources have been examined here. Chapter 5 is about the agricultural extension services that are needed for developing agribusiness. One related area, marketing of agricultural inputs is given in this unit. Agricultural marketing and processing activities are dealt in detail in Chapter 6. Chapter 7 makes a detailed analysis of the role of cooperatives agribusiness. The last Chapter explains the linkages of agro-processing with the national economy, export potential of agro-industries and the linkages of cooperatives with other sectors of the economy.

In preparing this book we have availed all resources—books, journals and website materials. Many of our friends gave us very good moral support to finish this work. We thank all those who stood with us. Last but not least, we express wholehearted thanks to the publishers for bringing this book neatly and in time. We leave the option to our readers and well-wishers to offer constructive comments, so that we can incorporate them in the next edition. We are thankful and grateful to Parul Wasan, Discovery Publishing House Pvt. Ltd., New Delhi for publishing the book neatly under his renowned label for the cooperative knowledge community.

S. NAKKIRAN
M. KARTHIKEYAN

Contents

1

Rural Economy and Agribusiness

MEANING AND SCOPE OF AGRIBUSINESS

Meaning

In agriculture, agribusiness is a generic term that refers to the various businesses involved in food production, including farming, seed supply, agrichemicals, farm machinery, wholesale and distribution, processing, marketing, and retail sales. The term has two distinctly different connotations depending on context.

Within the agriculture industry, agribusiness is widely used simply as a convenient portmanteau of agriculture and business, referring to the range of activities and disciplines encompassed by modern food production. Here, the term is only descriptive, and is synonymous in the broadest sense with food industry.

Among critics of large-scale, industrialized, vertically integrated food production, the term *agribusiness* is used as a negative, synonymous with corporate farming. Farming engaged in as a large-scale business operation embracing the production, processing, and distribution of agricultural products and the manufacture of farm machinery, equipment, and supplies. As such, it is often contrasted with family farm, a farm owned and operated by a family, and passed down from generation to generation. Some negative connotation is also derived from the negative associations of "business" and "corporation" from critics of capitalism or corporate excess.

Definitions

Dear Learner! Over the years the word agribusiness has evolved in its meaning and usage. Daniel Block has long felt that the broadest use of the word more truly reflects the diversity, complexity, technological sophistication and global scale of the agricultural economy of the 21st century.

Business dictionary defines Agribusiness as large-scale production, processing, and marketing of food and non-food farm commodities and products.

As of the definition of *Economics dictionary* "agribusiness are part of the economy devoted to the production, processing, and distribution of food, including the financial institutions that fund these activities."

Agribusiness emphasizes agriculture as a big business rather than as the work of small family farm.

Webster's Dictionary defines agribusiness as "farming and the business associated with farming, as the processing of farm products, the manufacturing of farm equipment and fertilizers, etc."

Block has defined agribusiness as, "any firm whose profits are dependent on or derived from the eventual harvest of agricultural production or natural resources. An agribusiness is uniquely characterized by its on-going need to adapt to several forces including; the biological phenomena of nature, weather conditions, changing consumer preferences for foods and fiber and the global supply and demand for the products of this harvest".

Thus the definition of agribusiness therefore includes three major sectors — Producers, Agricultural Input firms, and Agricultural Output firms. Due to the globalization and the industrialization of agriculture many large agribusiness companies today are vertically integrated and may include all three of these sectors.

Agribusiness Complex

Agribusiness management encompasses many aspects of the economy: agricultural producers, businesses that provide supplies and services to the producers (including cooperatives), businesses that add value to agricultural products, and those that facilitate the marketing of agricultural products to an ever-growing marketplace.

Agribusiness, also known as the Food and Fiber industry, is the chain of industries directly and indirectly involved in the production, transformation and provision of food, fiber, chemicals and pharmaceutical substrates.

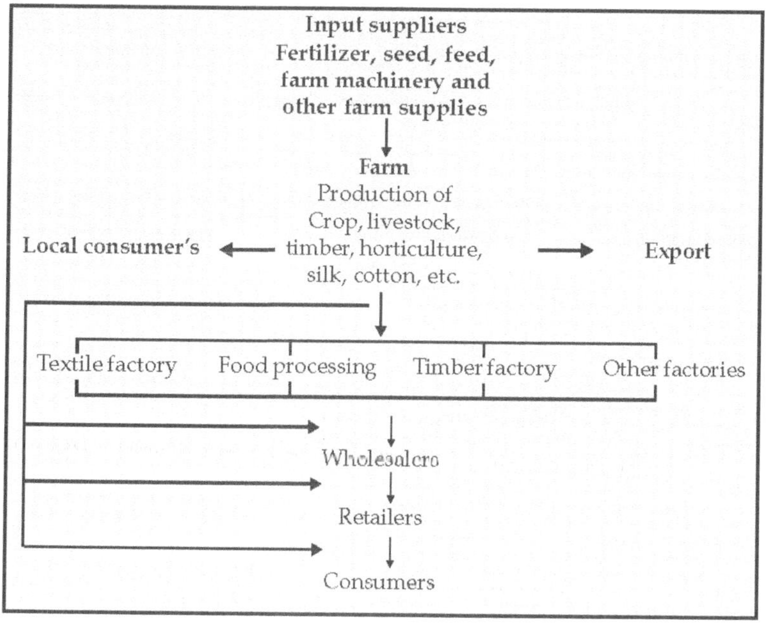

Fig. 1.1: **Major Sectors of Agribusiness**

At each level, there are brokers, transportation agents, financing firms that give special services to agribusiness.

Economic Sectors of Agribusiness

Agribusiness can be broken down into three economically interdependent sectors. These sectors are the input, farm and product sectors.

Farm Service Supply Industry/Agribusiness Input

The input sector or farm service supply industry transform minerals and other raw materials into farm machinery, fertilizer and other farm chemicals, and a variety of other commodities and services used in growing crops and raising livestock. In less developed countries this industry is generally small or poorly developed. The input sector also includes organizations engaged in the distribution of supplies like seed, feed, fertilizer, chemicals, machinery, and fuel and other inputs that is used for production of crops and livestock and providers of services in the production of agriculture like ploughing, planting, harvesting, vaccinating livestock, dehorning and other services.

Inputs are the various resources and services producers use to produce agricultural products. Using this definition, agribusiness firms include financial services companies, insurance providers, accountants and attorneys, as well as the more traditional agricultural input companies such as seed, feed, fertilizer, farm equipment, irrigation, animal pharmaceuticals, livestock handling equipment and horticultural supplies.

The growth of the farm supply industries is one of the important indicators of a country's stage of economic development. The products of these industries are used to increase the yield of crops and livestock and reduce the amount of land required to grow feed for work animals. This brings other changes in economic organization and management, on farms and elsewhere that save resources and release them for other uses. Labour requirement for farm production are reduced. As a general rule firms increase in size and scale as farming becomes a growing market for the products of the farm service supply industries and the increased production provides leads to the expansion of the agricultural processing and marketing industries.

Farm Sector/Agribusiness Producer

Farmer – Grower – Rancher - Aquacultures – Forestry – Fishing

Agribusiness includes the production sector of agriculture, traditionally referred to as the "the farmer". The farmer or producer today can be an individual grower, rancher or dairy farmer, a large, fresh produce grower/packer/shipper, an aquaculture company producing seafood, a forest product company growing trees, or an ornamental plant producer.

The farmer produces crops and animal products that are processed and distributed by the product/output sector to the final consumer. Professionally speaking the farming sector is referred as production agriculture. As the name implies production agriculture or a farm is an economic unit or a business firm organized to produce crops or raise livestock. Most people view that agriculture is another word for farming or ranching. But farming or ranching is one of the agricultural activities, which involve the activities of production of food and non-food products which are very important to us and to our economy. The food products include fruits, vegetables, cereals and beef. It also provides us the non- food products to our everyday life such as lumber, cotton, and wool and other products which have aesthetic and ornamental value like flower. Some times it is difficult to classify the products as food and non-food. Cotton, for instance, fits to both categories. The cotton fiber bale that is used to make cloth is a non-food item. But cotton seeds, among other things are used to make cooking oil and oleomargarine. If we take also fields of corn we think it is grown for us to eat but, corn is also grown to feed livestock. When corn is grown for animal consumption, it is classified as non-food product. Thus products which can be used for both purposes can be classified either way depending on how they are utilized.

Farming involves land, capital resources in addition to land management and labour. It requires a large fund and expanding industry, requiring continually increasing amounts of capital, advancing technology and more high level management. The capital requirements of modern farming are continuing to rise.

Modern farming is dynamic and growing, and it requires people with scientific training, management training and capability, ambition and skill, knowledge of economics, chemistry engineering, pathology, agronomy, entomology, genetics, nutrition and animal and soil science. The productivity per farm worker in countries where farming is most advanced is now several times as high as it was a short while ago. Continuing increases in productivity of farm workers result in more food being produced on a given amount of land with less labour.

Output Sector/Agribusiness Output

Finally, agribusiness includes the output side of agricultural production such as the post-harvest processing of vegetables, fruit, fiber, poultry and meats. Our definition of agribusiness output enterprises goes further to include the distributors, marketers, packagers, and retailers of agricultural food and fiber. It also includes firms involved in the post-harvest logistics of shipping and handling agricultural production such as the railroads, truckers, ocean carriers and airlines.

In general the output or agricultural processing—marketing industries includes businesses that add value to agricultural products, and those that facilitate the marketing of agricultural products to an ever-growing marketplace. The activities of the firms in this sector includes buy crops from farms and ranches, transporting, storing, processing, packaging and delivering the farm and ranch products and store where consumer buy.

The modern industrial economy is also characterized by a substantial development and growth of these industries, which in essence buy farm products and transform them into commodities suitable for consumption. In fact, the kind and amount of services added by these industries is also an indicator of a country's development and growth. In primitive or less developed countries much of the agriculture is used devoted to subsistence, and few services are added to farm products. The bulk of farm produce is delivered to consumers as unrefined food and fiber, unprocessed grain or livestock, or raw fruits and vegetables. As an economy develops, consumers demand more and more refinements in their food supply. They are willing to pay for more processing, increased convenience in terms of packaging, preserving, and freezing and enrichment of the product by various additives. Agricultural processing marketing industries grow because people are willing to pay for the services that are added. The modern supermarket offers a testimonial to the level of development in economy.

The agribusiness that process and market farm products include grain mills, meat packing dairy plants, food freezing firms, food drying and canning, manufacturing of fats and oils, lumber milling, grain barge lines, trucking firms, and railroad services. Every type of business or firms that add form and time utility or process or help market farm products is included in this category.

FEATURES OF RURAL ECONOMY OF ETHIOPIA

Ethiopian Economy – An Overview

Ethiopia is a country, which richly endowed with huge manpower, arable land and natural resource. However, much of its potential is not yet exploited. To start with, out of the sixty per cent of its landmass, which is known to have the potential for agricultural development, only 15 per cent is said to have been developed. Although its contribution to the national economy is very limited, the country's livestock wealth is the 2nd largest in Africa. The mineral resources' potential is also high, much of it yet to be exploited. According to studies, there are diverse mineral deposits in various parts of the country that can meet export standards. Minerals currently being exported include gold, platinum, marble, granite and tantalum. Export of these minerals is on a very limited scale relative to their immense export potential. Other metallic and non-metallic substances that have also been identified in the country include copper, lead, zinc, silver, gypsum, limestone, quartz and pyrite. Most Ethiopian mineral products are exportable to markets in East and Southern Africa and in Asia and Oceania. Due to freight costs, Ethiopian exports have an advantage in these regions of the world over established exports from Europe and North America. Ethiopia has also recently entered into the export of high quality dimensional stones (i.e., different types of unprocessed blocks, as well as processed marble, granite and limestone suitable for both internal and external uses.

The Ethiopian economy remains heavily dependent on agriculture, which accounts for about 50 per cent of the GDP. An estimated 85 per cent of the population gains its livelihood directly or indirectly from agricultural production. Coffee export accounts for more than 65 per cent of foreign exchange earnings, while processed and semi-processed hides and skins are the second important foreign exchange earners.

The level of the development of manufacturing sector in Ethiopia is at its infancy; and the country's industrial base is very low. The industrial sector is heavily dependent on imports of semi-processed goods, raw materials, spareparts and fuel. In addition to imported inputs the factories depend upon backward and subsistence agriculture for their raw material demand.

The industries include food processing and beverages, automotive industries which include production of components and parts, textile and textile products and garments, leather and leather products, fertilizers (mini-plant and chemicals), drugs and pharmaceuticals are some among others.

It is seen that over the years the largest contributor to GDP is the agricultural sector with nearly half of the share (Table 1.1). More significantly the sector accounts for 60 per cent of exports, and 80.2 per cent of total employment. The industry contribution to the GDP remains around 12-13 per cent which is the lowest of all the sectors. These figures emphasize the role of agricultural sector in economic development.

Table 1.1: Sector-wise contribution to GDP* of Ethiopia (In percentage share)

Sector	Year				
	1999-00	2000-01	2001-02	2002-03	2003-04
Agriculture	**48.2**	**49.8**	**48.8**	**44.8**	**47.4**
Crop	30.6	32.9	31.7	27.5	31.1
Livestock and hunting	12.0	11.6	11.6	11.4	10.9
Forestry	5.5	5.3	5.4	5.8	5.4
Fishing	0.04	0.04	0.04	0.05	0.04
Industry	**12.2**	**11.9**	**12.6**	**13.8**	**12.2**
Services	**39.5**	**38.4**	**38.6**	**41.5**	**39.5**
Total	**100.0**	**100.0**	**100.0**	**100.0**	**100.0**

* At constant factor cost of 1980-81.

Source: CSA, Ethiopia—Report on National Accounts, 2005.

In general, given the primary focus of the economy on agriculture and the diversity of crops and products, large-scale agro-processing offers numerous opportunities. Ethiopia's cash crop production has enormous potential for growth, especially in coffee, tea, sugar, spices, and tobacco. Cotton is well integrated in the economy with a large number of textile and garment factories relying on domestic production. Ethiopia already produces beeswax, oilseeds, fruits and vegetables for exports but there is plenty of room for growth. Another promising area is floriculture. With the increased growth of agricultural sector there is an increased scope for supporting and allied industries such as food processing, manufacturing of farm-equipment, fertilizers and other agro-chemicals. The cascading effect of all these activities is expected to result in faster development of the sector in particular and the economy in general.

Salient Features of Ethiopian Rural Economy

The salient features of Ethiopian Rural Economy can be described in the following ways. The following discussion will enable to understand the features:

Rural economy is not solely confined to agricultural activities, it embraces a number of activities outside agriculture. However, in the Ethiopian context, agriculture is central activity as the main means of livelihood. According to HICES (Household income expenditure survey-1999) results 73 per cent of total income source in rural areas is own agricultural enterprise, household enterprise other than agriculture 5.4, and wages and salaries 3.6. In the eastern and the southern arid and semi-arid areas, the peoples main sources of livelihood is cattle herding, the western lowlands large uncultivated land and low population density and in the highlands, there is limited farmland along with high population density. As mentioned earlier majority of Ethiopia population resides in the rural area mainly depending its life on agriculture according to MEDaC (1999) where the countries economy highly depends. The agriculture and allied activity comprises proper agriculture (crop and livestock), forestry and fishing. Crop production is estimated to contribute on the average around 60 per cent, livestock accounts for about 27 per cent and other sub-sectors 13 per cent of the total agriculture value added (MEDaC 1999). In spite of its importance in the national economy, agriculture is largely based on subsistence farm household, whose modes of life and work have remained unchanged for centuries. Although the majority of the Ethiopian labour force is employed in agriculture yet the sector has not been able to satisfy the food requirements of the people. There are so serious problems associated with chronic food insecurity that millions of people need food assistance and thousands die of starvation.

Table 1.2 shows that the great majority (about 83%) of holders of agricultural land in the country holds crop area of size 2 hectares or less which probably can be categorized as small and marginal. It is also to be noted that the average size of holdings is 1.20 hectares for all holders and such farm holdings may be scattered over a large geographical area.

Resources

(a) Crop resources

Crop growth and development are primarily governed by environment conditions of soil and weather. The success or failure of farming, and quantitative and qualitative improvement in crop production are intimately related to the prevailing weather conditions. Vagaries of weather phenomena also affect agriculture by interfering with routine agricultural operation and plant protection measures. Further, influence of weather on crop growth and yield depends on crop growth stage. Crops are often influenced significantly by a few weather factors for their growth and development.

Ethiopia is endowed with a variety of agro-ecological zones that are different in terms of rainfall pattern, soil types, altitude and other physical landscapes which allows numerous crop species to be grown. These different agro-ecological zones in the country imply that many different agricultural products can be produced in the different regions. As an agro-ecological zone that is suitable for a given product may not be conducive for another.

The farming system can be classified into the smallholder farming system, pastoral-nomadic system, and commercial farming system however the sector is dominated by small-scale farmers who have been adopting rain-fed mixed farming with traditional technology where the productivity of farming is highly dependent in the prevailing weather condition. Small-scale farmers on the average account for about 90 per cent of the total area under crop production and for more than 90 per cent of the total agricultural output.

Table 1.2: Distribution of total number of holders, total crop area and crop area per holder by size of holding, main season 2004-05 Ethiopia

No. of holders and area	Size of holding (Hectares)							
	0.00-0.10	0.10-0.50	0.51-1.00	1.01-2.00	2.01-5.00	5.01-10.00	10.01+	Total
Number of holders	750,938	2,791,556	2,778,223	3,010,777	1,836,183	156,308	11,966	11,335,945
Cumulative per cent of holders	6.62	31.25	55.76	82.32	98.52	100.00	100.00	100.00
Total crop area (hectare)	23,679	683,346	1,708,627	3,588,243	4,158,135	650,841	75,083	10,887,953
Cumulative per cent of total crop area	0.22	6.49	22.19	55.14	93.33	100.00	100.00	100.00
Average crop area per holder (hectare)	0.05	0.30	0.74	1.43	2.86	6.39	13.11	1.20

Source: CSA, Ethiopia—Report on Agriculture, 2005.

Moreover 94 per cent of food crops and 98 per cent of coffee produced by small-scale farmers while the remaining 6 per cent of food crops and 2 per cent coffee are generated from commercial farmers (state and private).

Studies suggest that on the average, small landholding is around 1.2 hectare per household. Most of the small plot of land is devoted to food crop production but households seldom produce enough crops to meet their family's consumption requirement. As the land is too small to produce any marketable surplus under the prevailing conditions, subsistence and survival are the overriding concern of the farmers. This resulted in lack of cash for investment, purchase of commercial inputs and purchase of oxen for land preparation.

The major crop categories produced by the country in accordance with CSA classification are cereals, pulses and oilseeds. The principal cereal crops are teff, barely, wheat, maize, sorghum, millet, and oats. Pulses include horse bean, chick peas, haricot beans, field peas, lentils and vetch. And oilseeds or others include neug, linseed, fenugreek, rapeseed, sunflower, groundnuts, and sesame. The most important cash crop in Ethiopia was coffee. Approximately 25 per cent of Ethiopia's population depended directly or indirectly on coffee for its livelihood.

(b) Livestock resources

Livestock is the integral part of all farming systems in Ethiopia. In the eastern and southern arid and semi-arid areas it is the main source of livelihood. About 15 per cent of the country's population is pastoral. They move seasonally with their herds of livestock (mainly goat, sheep, cattle, and camel) to find water and forage. Pastoral region represents approximately 60 per cent of the country's land mass and are among the most inaccessible. Livestock serves as source of draught power and cash income for the large majority of the Ethiopian rural population, which is engaged in farming.

Livestock also provides milk and meat to both rural and urban population. Manure from livestock is an important fuel and fertilizer while hides and skins are important for local leather-based industries as well as export.

In Ethiopia livestock rearing is subsistence type and usually not oriented towards the production of marketable surplus. Even though Ethiopia in terms of livestock possession stands first in Africa and tenth in the world according to MOA, due to the prevalence of livestock disease the country loses about 8.10 per cent of cattle, 14.16 per cent of sheep and 11.1 per cent of goats per year. Moreover, the numerous livestock in the country lacks high quality and productivity. Cows do not reach maturity until 3.5–4 years of age and produce 250–300 liters of milk per lactation (Eth. 1996). The unit weights are among the lowest in Africa. But studies confirm that some local cattle breeds such as the Borena, Fogera, Barka, and Horo have high potential for milk production.

(c) *Land and water resources*

As earlier it is mentioned that Ethiopian economy is highly dependent on agriculture and the first thing that comes to our mind while talking about agriculture is land. In fact, it is not possible to think of agriculture without the use of land. The use of land in non-agricultural pursuits is not less significant but the nature of agricultural industry and its various processes make the use of land central to the agricultural pursuits. Land is the basis of agriculture and in general virtually all types of production depends on land and all agricultural production depends on it in particular. The concept of land in economics is very complex and is held to stand for all natural resources. Land in agriculture may however be used in restricted sense though its complex form affects agriculture in several ways. To be precise we are discussing pertinent to farmland. Besides being the resources for crop, fodder, and forest production, it also provides space for building cities, roads, airports, health resorts, schools, industries and so on. So as far the role of land in agriculture is concerned, it serves as the source of food and fiber production, pastures and grazing lands and forests.

The size of Ethiopia is 111.5 million ha. Out of this, 74 million ha or 66 per cent of the total area is suitable for agriculture. However, actual size of land cultivated is estimated to be only 16.5 million ha or 14.8 per cent of the total. Topographically and climatically the land of Ethiopia is divided into regions of western highlands and lowlands; southern highlands and lowlands, and central rift valley between the two sets of highlands. The large tracts of land with low population density is particularly found in the western lowlands stretching from north to south, which are suitable for agricultural development under some conditions like irrigation development and other measures after assessing prevailing conditions. These areas can become areas of commercial farming and will have a significant impact on the country's overall economic development.

Ethiopia is well known for its water resources and she is known as the water tower of north-east Africa. Surface water resources in the country flow in the major river basins where the rift valley is the region of the great inland rivers of Awash, Bilete, and Gibe-Omo and lakes of Ziway, Langano, Abyata, Shala, Awasa, Abaya, Chamo and Chewbahir. The country's total ground water are estimated to be around 2.6 billion m^3. The wet land in the various parts of the country covers a total of 18,587km^3 which is estimated to be 1.5 per cent of the country's area. From the total surface water resources of the country 80 to 90 per cent of the resources are found in the river basins of Abay, Tekeze, Baro and Omo-Gibe. An estimated 30 to 40 per cent of the countries population live in these basins. On the other hand, estimated population of the country to be 60 to 70 which live in eastern and central Ethiopia only 10 to 20 per cent of the total volume of the country's water resource is estimated to be located. While the country is endowed with water resource it is estimated that there are 3.5 million hectares of land has the potential to be irrigated in the river basins. Even though the countries potential irrigable land as compared to other forty-four African countries puts the country in the fourth place however the actual utilization of the water resources for irrigation puts the country at the eleventh position.

Trade

As the Ethiopian economy is highly dependent on agriculture the export products of the country is dominated by agricultural products. These export products rely heavily on agricultural products that originate mainly from smallholder peasant farming. The major export products include coffee, hides, skin and leather products, textile and garments, cereal, pulses and oilseed; meat products and live cattle; fruits and vegetable, cut flower. Other export commodities include spices, civet, beverages, beeswax, gall-stone and fish.

Major imports include: Aircraft; motor vehicles, agricultural and industrial machinery, equipment and spare parts; chemicals and pharmaceuticals; petroleum products; food products; garments and footwear; building materials.

(a) Coffee

Being the origin of coffee arabica, Ethiopia has immense potential to offer the world market a wide variety of flavors of organically produced, washed and sun-dried coffee. Flavors range from the fruity flavor of Ghimbi to the winery flavor of Limu to the cheesy flavor of Illubabor to the mocha flavors of Yirga cheffe and Harar. Today, coffee consumers worldwide are appreciating the value of organic coffee's natural aroma and flavor. More than 90 per cent of the coffee harvested in Ethiopia is organically grown. The inherently superior quality of Ethiopian highland arabica coffee is unmatched, particularly in flavor and aroma. Ethiopia also produces several types of coffee, the water soluble extracts of which can be used for hot beverages, iced drinks, ice creams and in the confectionary industry.

(b) *Leather and leather products*

Ethiopia offers a wide range of processed and semi-processed hides and skins to the world market. Some of the products, such as Ethiopian highland sheepskin (which has gained an international reputation for making gloves), are known for their quality and natural characteristics. Ethiopian hide and skin exports include pickled sheep skin, wet blue sheep skin, crust sheep skin, wet blue goat skin, crust goat skin, crust cow hides, finished garment leather, finished glove leather, lining/upper leather, suede leather, full grain leather, embossed leather and patent leather. The export of finished leather and leather products (such as leather garments, footwear, gloves, bags and other leather articles) is also highly promising.

(c) *Live animals and meat*

With the largest livestock population in Africa, Ethiopia has an ample supply base for the export of live animals and meat. Its livestock resources are estimated at 27 million cattle, 24 million sheep and 18 million goats. Livestock husbandry is mostly carried out under natural grazing, making the meat and meat products obtained from the animals are very tasty and nutritionally healthy for human consumption. Ethiopia's main exports of live animals and meat products include steers and yearlings; lowland sheep and goats; fresh and chilled lamb and mutton carcass; fresh and chilled goat carcass; fresh and chilled veal carcass and beef four quarter; fresh and chilled boneless veal and beef; frozen lamb, mutton and goat carcass and veal and beef special cuts.

(d) *Textile fabrics and garments*

The textile industry is the largest manufacturing industry in the country. There are more than fourteen major state-owned and private textile and garment factories. The industry employs about 30,000 workers and represents 36 per cent of the entire manufacturing industry. The main textile products manufactured in the country are cotton and nylon fabrics, acrylic yarn, woolen and waste cotton blankets and sewing thread. The domestic potential of cotton production as basic raw material is far more than the demand of the currently installed spinning capacity and the availability of cheap labour is one of the major parameters for considering this industrial sector as one of the strategic industries for export development.

(e) *Oilseeds and pulses*

Ethiopian oilseeds and pulses are known for their flavor and nutritional value as they are mostly produced organically. For instance, the Ethiopian white sesame seed is used as a reference for grading in international markets. In terms of quantity, in 1996-97, for example, Ethiopia exported 87 thousand tons of oilseeds and 20 thousand tons of pulses. Ethiopia's major oilseed and pulse exports include sesame seeds, nigger seeds, linseeds, sunflower seeds, groundnuts, rapeseeds, castor oil seeds, pumpkin seeds, haricot beans, pea-beans, horse beans and chick peas. Saudi Arabia, Yemen, Israel, EU countries, and some Asian and neighboring African countries constitute the major markets for Ethiopia's oilseeds and pulse exports.

(f) *Fruits, vegetables and flowers*

With a favorable climate, abundant labour, land and water resources, most regions of the country are suitable for the production of a wide range of tropical and sub-tropical fruits, vegetables and flowers. The major vegetable export products include potatoes, green beans, okra, melon, white and red onions, shallots, cabbage, leeks, beetroot, carrots, green chilies, tomatoes and lettuce. The main exportable fruits include oranges, mandarin grapefruit, mangos, guavas, lemons and limes, while cut flower exports include statice, allium, roses and carnations.

(g) *Tea*

The quality of tea mainly depends on climatic conditions, the type of soil upon which the plant grows and the method of processing. In Ethiopia, tea is mostly grown in the highland dense forest regions where the land is fertile and thus the use of fertilizer is very minimal. Moreover, the availability of abundant and cheap labour in the country has made the use of manual weeding, instead of chemical *seeding*, possible. Because of this mostly organic cultivation, Ethiopian tea is increasingly sought for its aroma and natural flavors.

(*h*) *Natural gum*

Ethiopia is endowed with distinct climatic conditions that enable it to grow diverse plant species, which are used for industrial and pharmaceutical purposes. Acacia, Commiphora and Boswellia are examples of one group of plant species that grows in the arid and semi-arid areas yielding gum. The increasing consumption of convenience foods has enhanced the growth of gum production and use over the past several years. As in most other sectors of the additive industry, increasing health consciousness has tended to fuel the demand for thickeners of natural origin. The major gum products produced mainly for export are gum olibanum derived from boswellia, gum myrrh and oppoponex derived from commiphora and gum Arabic derived from acacia species. Apart from their pharmaceutical applications, these products have a wide-range of industrial uses in such areas as beverages, candies, chewing gum, confectionaries, dairy products, gelatins, nut products, puddings and canned vegetables. Typical applications for gum products include: adhesive thickeners; thickeners, stabilizers, flavor, fixatives and emulsifying agents in food products; clarification in beverages; release agents for rubber products and formulations in cosmetics.

Rural Infrastructure

Accurate data on the location, type, and quality of roads in Ethiopia is not well known this is partly because road works and conditions are constantly changing over time and across seasons. However it is well known that much of the country is poorly serviced by roads. This is true not only for the sparsely populated areas of the arid eastern lowlands, but also for much of highly populated areas of the highlands. According to World Bank (2000) Ethiopia has 12 per cent paved road.

The rural areas of Ethiopia is determined as inaccessible by transportation means where studies shows that more than 75 per cent of farms are more than half a day walk away from an all weather road. Agricultural inputs and outputs are transported by traditional transport means like pack animals or humans. The poor rural infrastructure affects market efficiency of the rural area. The sale of farm products is confined to the village market specially, perishable agricultural products which are easily deteriorate and require quick marketing.

Access to telephone service in Ethiopia is very limited. In almost half of the country's zones there are more than 70 households for every fixed telephone line operating in that zone. A fixed line refers to the physical capacity to enable a residential, commercial, or public telephone using a cable connection (this does not include mobile/cellular phones). Almost one-third of the zones have more than 200 households per fixed line; 12 zones have no telephone service at all. Although some telephone service centers are located in remote areas, they are mostly concentrated along all-weather roads in the highlands. As with other services, many rural residents live quite a distance from the nearest telephone.

There is relatively better access to postal services across the country than to other communication services. The patterns of access vary, but they correspond somewhat to the size of the urban center and locations of major roads: the majority of post offices tend to be located in larger settlements and towns on major roads.

Cooperatives provide an important institutional arrangement that can enhance smallholder opportunities for acquiring and responding to information about new technologies and market opportunities. The relatively diffuse spread of cooperatives throughout the most productive highland areas is high. Coffee and cereal cooperatives are prominent in terms of both geographic spread and size of membership. Multipurpose cooperatives provide production and marketing assistance for a variety of commodities (honey, oilseeds, grains, and so on) and also are widely distributed in this zone. Tigray, southern portions of SNNP, and southeastern Oromia have relatively few cooperatives compared with the number of smallholders in these areas. Cooperatives are absent in the lowland areas.

Table 1.3: Technology and Infrastructure Status of Ethiopia

Indicator	Value	Source
Paved roads (% of total)	12.0	World Bank (2000)
Radios (per 1000 people)	196	UNECA (1995)
Fixed lines and mobile telephones (per 1000 people)	3.9	World Bank (2000)
Telecommunications lines in urban areas (%)	95	UNECA (2001)
TVs (per 1000 people)	6	UNECA (2000)
Number of personal computers (per 1000 people)	0.9	World Bank (2000)
Number of Internet users	25,000	UNECA (2001)

Savings and investment plays key roles in speeding up economic growth, expanding employment opportunities and improving the people's standard of living. Microfinance institutions are a source of access to financial credit for smallholders. Loans are typically made for the purchase of inputs (fertilizer, fungicides, herbicides, and so on), capital acquisition (livestock, machinery, buildings), or other improvements. Microfinance institutions typically differ from banks in that they offer smaller loans, thereby making credit more accessible to farmers. It shows that rural borrowing is much more concentrated in the central highlands, especially eastern Tigray and Amhara, than elsewhere. There are also government and private banks in the country. In rural areas, the banks are located in the center of each woreda in which one or more banks have an office. While both private and government banks have wide branch-office distributions, they tend to cluster along all-weather roads. Moreover, compared to government banks, private banks rarely have branch offices in rural locations off main roads.

Education

In the last two decades, encouraging results have been obtained in-terms of enrollment at all educational levels. Especially, the past five years have exhibited substantial improvement in the education sector. During the recent five years (2000/01-2005/06), the Gross Enrollment Ratio (GER) of primary 1st cycle (Grades 1-4) increased by 24.6 per cent while that of the 2nd cycle (Grades 5-8) has increased by 28 per cent. The GER at primary level (grades 1-8) has reached 85.8 per cent and the Net Enrollment Ratio (NER) 73.9 per cent. The gender gap has also narrowed from 20.3 per cent in 2000/01 to 14.4 per cent in 2005/06 showing a reduction of 5.9 per cent. This shows an increasing trend in girls education which is expected to contribute a lot to socio-economic development. Although millions of Ethiopian children are part of the education system significant share of the primary school-age populations still are not enrolled. Rapid population growth, which results in increasing the size of the school-age population, continuous challenging the government's effort of meeting one of the Millennium Development Goals (MDGs) i.e., universal primary education for all by 2015.

Demography

Supply of labour force in agriculture depends upon the size of the population. In traditional static agriculture, the size of farm labour force directly varied with the size of total population. Alternative employment avenues being nonexistent, an increase in population straight forward led to increase in labour force in farm sector and vice versa. In the event of farm and non-farm sectors existing side by side, agricultural labour force depend upon the residual formed by the rate of growth of population and the rate of growth of non-agricultural employment.

Transformation from traditional static agriculture to dynamic agriculture depends as much upon the farm labour force as on the technological innovations. Farm labour has been a pivotal point in the models of economic development in general, and in agricultural development in particular. The history of economic transition suggests that over a long period of time, the pressure of population on land increased considerably. Land being limited, with every increase in population, the man and land ratio went on increasing and consequently remuneration per unit of labour declined accordingly till it become at the subsistence level since it couldn't go beyond below that. In the absence of alternative employment due to non-existence or relatively small size of non-farm sector, agriculture had to absorb the shocks of additional manpower, rendering, in the process, a sizable amount of farm labour as redundant.

The Ethiopian population is estimated at 75 million in mid-July 2006 with a growth rate of 2.62 per cent per annum (approximately additional 2 million people per year). From the total population, 50.1 per cent are males and 49.9 per cent are females. Considering the age structure of the population, 43 per cent is under the age of fifteen which shows high level of dependency burden and elevated potential for rapid population growth. The share of working age (15-64 years) population is 54.2 and that of the old age population (>65 years) is estimated at 2.8 per cent.

In Ethiopia, population distribution is highly uneven. The overwhelming majority (84%) resides in rural areas where agriculture is a predominant economic activity, infrastructure and social services are not well developed. Only 16 per cent of the population is urban dwellers. Population density is varied and follows altitudinal and agroecological lines. The highlands (*dega*) are the most densely populated, while the lowlands (*k'olla*) have the lowest population densities.

Ethiopia's agricultural sector which is dominated by small-holder farmers is based on family labour. This situation requires that the formulation of agricultural policies in the country should aim at influencing the inputs, outputs and technology of farm household production. In other words, in Ethiopia where agriculture makes up a large proportion of the labour force and prospects for expansion of non-farm employment are limited, the labour-intensive approach may be an appropriate choice to increase the productivity of the agricultural sector and it should be supported with the adoption of new agricultural technologies and the training of the agricultural labour force with effective skills. However the landholding of farmers of Ethiopia is less than one hectare or small-scale farmers dominate the agricultural sector which may require policy that changes the landholding of the farmer to utilize the available large labour resource and non-farm employment opportunity to absorb the highly increasing population.

Employment Status

In 2003 employment status shows, 50.3 and 40.9 per cent of the employed population aged 10 years and above of the country were unpaid family workers and self-employed (own account workers), respectively. The paid employee altogether constituted only about 8.0 per cent of the total working population. In rural areas, the percentage of the unpaid family workers make up 54.6 per cent. Higher proportion of paid employees (42.8%) were found in urban areas and small proportion (3.6%) in rural areas.

The Occupational Group result of the 2005 NLFS data showed that, at country level the highest proportion (42.8%) of employed persons are engaged in elementary occupations. Elementary occupation mainly includes daily labourers in agriculture, mining and construction. Next to this occupational group are persons engaged in skilled agricultural and fishery occupation, constituting 40.5 per cent of the total employed persons. Crafts and related trade and service and market sales workers make up about 7.0 per cent and 6.7 per cent of the country's total employed persons, respectively.

Employment status as industrial divisions overall, agriculture, which includes crop production, animal husbandry, hunting, forestry and fishing make up 80.2 per cent of all industries of the employed person. Wholesale and retail trade, took a share of 5.2 per cent at country level. The share of hotels and restaurants was 2.5 per cent. On the other hand, 21.8 per cent of the employed persons in urban areas were engaged in the wholesale and retail trades, followed by manufacturing (14.3%), education, health and other social activities (14.1%), agriculture, hunting, forestry and fishing (13.0%) and hotel and restaurant (10.8%).

PLACE OF AGRIBUSINESS IN RURAL ECONOMY OF ETHIOPIA

This section discusses about place of agribusiness in rural economy. We have to understand the place of agribusiness in the rural economy through understanding of agriculture, modern agriculture and the Eras coming under it. Agribusiness has its own place and share in agriculture. The place of agribusiness in rural economy is mainly discussed in this point of view hereunder.

The word agriculture is the English adaptation of Latin term *agricultûra*, which is derived from two words *ager*, 'a field', and *cultûra*, 'cultivation' in the strict sense of "tillage of the soil". Thus, a literal reading of the word yields "tillage of a field/of fields". However agriculture includes far more than tilling of a field or the raising of field crops. It includes animal husbandry, tree culture, forestry, irrigation, fish hatcheries, full farming, and other varied activities. Food getting constitutes by far the most essential and largest function of agriculture; but after all, the production of fibers, tobacco, inedible fats, wood pulp, and so on is agriculture too. In general agriculture refers to the production of goods through the growing of plants, animals and other life forms. The study of agriculture is known as agricultural science.

Agriculture is defined as the art or science of cultivating the ground including the harvesting of crops, and the rearing and management of live stock; tillage; husbandry; farming.

Agriculture science, art or business

The following discussion will enable you to understand that agriculture is a business i.e., agribusiness. The place of agribusiness in rural economy can be understood in this sense.

Agriculture can be termed as science, art, or business altogether. Agriculture is seen as a science, because it employs scientific skills to develop new strains of crops—trees, animals, fish and birds and develops innovate techniques to manage them under varying soil and environmental conditions. As an art it is the management whether it is the management of crops, animals, birds, fish or any other branch of agriculture that brings about desired results. Agriculture is also a business because the entire produce and inputs of agriculture are linked with marketing which brings in the question of profit and loss. As such, agriculture is a very comprehensive applied science dealing with all aspects of life.

Agriculture encompasses many subjects, including aquaculture, agronomy, animal husbandry, and horticulture.

Aquaculture

Aquaculture is the cultivation of aquatic organisms. Unlike fishing, aquaculture, also known as "aquafarming", implies the cultivation of aquatic populations under controlled conditions. "Mariculture" refers to aquaculture practiced in marine environments. Particular kinds of aquaculture include algaculture (the production of kelp/seaweed and other algae); fish farming; shrimp farming, shellfish farming, and the growing of cultured pearls.

Fish farming is the principal form of aquaculture, while other methods may fall under mariculture. It involves raising fish commercially in tanks or enclosures, usually for food. A facility that releases juvenile fish into the wild for recreational fishing or to supplement a species' natural numbers is generally referred to as a fish hatchery.

Increasing demands on wild fisheries by commercial fishing operations have caused widespread overfishing. Fish farming offers an alternative solution to the increasing market demand for fish and fish protein.

Agronomy

Agronomy is the science of utilizing plants for food, fuel, feed, and fiber. To do this effectively and in a sustainable manner, agronomy encompasses work in the areas of plant genetics, plant physiology, meteorology, and soil science. Agronomy is the application of a combination of sciences like biology, chemistry, ecology, earth science, and genetics. Agronomists today are involved with many issues including producing food, creating healthier food, managing environmental impacts, and creating energy from plants. Agronomists often specialize in areas such as crop rotation, irrigation and drainage, plant breeding, soil classification, soil fertility, weed control, insect and pest control and other areas.

Animal husbandry

Animal husbandry, also called animal science, stockbreeding or simple husbandry, is the agricultural practice of breeding and raising livestock.

The word horticulture is a 17th century English adaptation of the Latin *hortus* (garden) and *cultura* (culture). Horticulture is the art of gardening or plant growing, in contrast to agronomy — the cultivation of field crops such as cereals and animal fodder, forestry — cultivation of trees and products related to them, or agriculture — the practice of farming.

Horticulture

Horticulture is the art and science of the cultivation of plants. Horticulture sometimes differs from agriculture in:

1. a smaller scale of cultivation, using small plots of mixed crops rather than large field of single crops;
2. the cultivation of a wider variety of crops, often including fruit trees.

Horticulture involves six areas of study, which can be grouped into two broad sections — ornamentals and edibles.

Arboriculture

The study and selection, planting, care, and removal of individual trees, shrubs, vines, and other perennial woody plants.

Arboriculture is the cultivation of trees and shrubs. The discipline includes the study of how they grow and respond to cultural practices and the environment as well as aspects of cultivation such as selection, planting, care, and removal.

The purpose is generally to manage amenity trees. That is trees where their value to the landscape is greater than that of their wood content. Trees offer environmental benefits as well as cultural, heritage and habitat for fauna. The combined value including aesthetics exceeds the value of a trees worth from a forestry wood perspective. Amenity trees are usually in a garden or urban setting, and arboriculture is the management of them for plant health and longevity, pest and pathogen resistance, risk management and ornamental or aesthetic reasons. In this, it needs to be distinguished from forestry, which is the commercial production and use of timber and other forest products from plantations and forests. Arboriculture can be considered to have a similar relationship to forestry.

Floriculture

Floriculture (includes production and marketing of floral crops).

Floriculture, or flower farming, is a discipline of horticulture concerned with the cultivation of flowering and ornamental plants for gardens and for floristry, comprising the floral industry. The development of plant breeding of new varieties is a major occupation of floriculturists.

Floriculture crops include bedding plants, flowering plants, foliage plants or houseplants, cut cultivated greens, and cut flowers. As distinguished from nursery crops, floriculture crops are generally herbaceous. Bedding and garden plants consist of young flowering plants (annuals and perennials) and vegetable plants. They are grown in cell packs (in flats or trays), in pots, or in hanging baskets, usually inside a controlled environment, and sold largely for gardens and landscaping.

Flowering plants are largely sold in pots for indoor use. The major flowering plants are poinsettias, orchids, florist chrysanthemums, and finished florist azaleas. Foliage plants are also sold in pots and hanging baskets for indoor and patio use, including larger specimens for office, hotel, and restaurant interiors.

Cut flowers are usually sold in bunches or as bouquets with cut foliage. The production of cut flowers is specifically known as the cut flower industry. Farming flowers and foliage employs special aspects of floriculture, such as spacing, training and pruning plants for optimal flower harvest; and post-harvest treatment such as chemical treatments, storage, preservation and packaging. In Australia and the United States some species are harvested from the wild for the cut flower market.

Landscape horticulture

Landscape horticulture includes production, marketing and maintenance of landscape plants.

Landscape architecture is the art, planning, design, management, preservation and rehabilitation of the land and the design of human-made constructs. The scope of the profession includes architectural design, site planning, housing estate development, environmental restoration, town or urban planning, urban design, parks and recreation planning, regional planning, landscape urbanism, and historic preservation.

Olericulture

Olericulture is the science of vegetable growing, dealing with the culture of non-woody (herbaceous) plants for food (includes production and marketing of vegetables). Olericulture is the production of plants for use of the edible parts. Vegetable crops can be classified into 9 major categories:

- Potherbs and greens — spinach and collards
- Salad crops — lettuce, celery
- Cole crops — cabbage and cauliflower
- Root/tuber crops — potatoes, beets, carrots, radishes
- Bulb crops — onions, leeks
- Legumes — beans, peas
- Cucurbits — melons, squash, cucumber
- Solanaceous crops - tomatoes, peppers

Olericulture deals with the production, storage, processing and marketing of vegetables. It encompasses crop establishment, including cultivar selection, seedbed preparation and establishment of vegetable crops by seed and transplants. It also includes maintenance and care of vegetable crops as well commercial and non-traditional vegetable crop production including organic, sustainable horticulture, hydroponics and biotechnology.

Pomology

Pomology includes production and marketing of fruits.

The word Pomology derived from Latin *pomum* (fruit) and *logy (study)*. It is the branch of botany that studies and cultivates fruits.

The pomological researches are mainly focused on the development of and the cultural techniques and physiological studies in fruit trees. The goals of fruit tree improvement include enhancement of fruit quality, regulation of production periods, and reduction of production cost.

Postharvest physiology

Postharvest physiology involves in maintaining quality and preventing spoilage of horticultural crops.

Postharvest physiology is a field which studies maintaining quality and preventing spoilage of horticultural crops. In agriculture, *postharvest handling* is the stage of crop production immediately following harvest, including cooling, cleaning, sorting and packing. The instant a crop is removed from the ground, or separated from its parent plant, it begins to deteriorate. Postharvest treatment largely determines final quality, whether a crop is sold for fresh consumption, or used as an ingredient in a processed food product.

The most important goals of post-harvest handling are keeping the product cool, to avoid moisture loss and slow down undesirable chemical changes, and avoiding physical damage such as bruising, to delay spoilage. Sanitation is also an important factor, to reduce the possibility of pathogens that could be carried by fresh produce, for example, as residue from contaminated washing water.

After the field, post-harvest processing is usually continued in a packing house. This can be a simple shed, providing shade and running water, or a large-scale, sophisticated, mechanized facility, with conveyor belts, automated sorting and packing stations, walk-in coolers and the like. In mechanized harvesting, processing may also begin as part of the actual harvest process, with initial cleaning and sorting performed by the harvesting machinery.

Initial post-harvest storage conditions are critical to maintaining quality. Each crop has an optimum range for storage temperature and humidity. Also, certain crops cannot be effectively stored together, as unwanted chemical interactions can result. Various methods of high-speed cooling, and sophisticated refrigerated and atmosphere-controlled environments, are employed to prolong freshness, particularly in large-scale operations.

Regardless of the scale of harvest, from home garden to industrialized farm, the basic principles of post-harvest handling for most crops are the same:

- handle with care to avoid damage (cutting, crushing, bruising)
- cool immediately and maintain in cool conditions
- cull (remove damaged items)

AGRIBUSINESS AND HISTORICAL ORIGIN OF AGRICULTURE

The historical origin of agriculture reveals the place of agibusiness in rural economy. The following discussion makes you to understand the concept.

The history of agriculture is a central element of human history, as agricultural progress has been a crucial factor in worldwide socio-economic change. Wealth-building and militaristic specializations rarely seen in hunter-gatherer cultures are commonplace in agricultural and agro-industrial societies—when farmers became capable of producing food beyond the needs of their own families, others in the tribe/village/city-state/nation/empire were freed to devote themselves to projects other than food acquisition. Jared Diamond, among others, has argued that the development of civilization required agriculture.

As of 2006, an estimated 36 per cent of the world's workers are employed in agriculture (down from 42% in 1996). However, the relative significance of farming has dropped steadily since the beginning of industrialization, and in 2006 — for the first time in history — the services sector overtook agriculture as the economic sector employing the most people worldwide. Despite the fact that agriculture employs over one-third of the world's population, agricultural production accounts for less than five per cent of the gross world product (an aggregate of all gross domestic products).

Views in the origin of agriculture are diverse from mythological to ecological. Whatever promoted humans to purposely raise their plants in a specific area and confine their animals did not likely happen overnight. It was an evolutionary process that eventually transformed plants from being independent, wild progenitors, to fully dependent and domesticated cultivars, with the concomitant evolution of agricultural economies.

Various mythologies suggest that agriculture is a divine gift to men. Others explain that the shift from nomadic lifestyle to sedentary plant and animal culture was necessitated by religious obligations, which required animals and certain plants to be kept for ritual sacrifice to gods. The Propinquity Theory of Gordon Childe suggests that wild animals, and for the matter plants, were forced into closer cohabitation when advancing dry climatic conditions pushed humans animals into more habitable areas such as the bank of perennial rivers. This is also referred to as the "Theory of Domestication by Crowding".

Of all the views of agricultural origins, suggesting agriculture as an invention and discovery appears to be the most enduring. There are various views as to how this discovery was made. Charles Darwin suggested that first humans had to become sedentary for this discovery to occur. By products of their lifestyle, specifically garbage had to be disposed of in a refuse dump near their habitation. Out of this discarded heap of waste, seeds from a useful plant (that had been previously gathered for food or medicine) are likely to have germinated and grown in the fertile soils of the refuse dump to produce bountifully. Some wise person was bound to have made the observation of these plants and the connection between planting seeds and producing desired plants in a certain location in the vicinity of his or her abode. This is the "plant domestication by happy accident model".

Carl Sauer further developed this story. It was suggested that not only did the inventors of agriculture have to be sedentary, primitive agriculturalists were most likely to have hailed from fishing communities. Such communities had to be located in wooded lands where it was relatively easier to till the soil, not having to contend with the soil binding effect of grass roots in grasslands. Further, these discoveries would have previously acquired certain skills in other aspects of living in the wild that would predispose them to agricultural experimentation.

From this and other presuppositions, the most likely candidate for an area of origin of agriculture was Southeast Asia, from where it spread to China, India, the Near East, Africa, the Mediterranean, and lastly North and West Europe. Edgar Anderson later strengthened the Sauer model with genetic recombinants from which useful selections could be found.

EVOLUTION OF MODERN AGRICULTURE

Crop production has not always been what it is today. How it changed over the years? Agriculture was developed at least 10,000 years ago, and it has undergone significant developments since the time of the earliest cultivation. Evidences points to the Fertile Crescent of the Middle East as the site of the earliest planned sowing and harvesting of plants that had previously been gathered in the wild. Independent development of agriculture occurred in northern and southern China, Africa's Sahel, New Guinea and several regions of the Americas. Modern agriculture benefits from research and technological advancement. As economics permits, producers are able to implement new techniques and technologies to facilitate agricultural production.

Agricultural practices such as irrigation, crop rotation, fertilizers, and pesticides were developed long ago but have made great strides in the past century. The Haber-Bosch method for synthesizing ammonium nitrate represented a major breakthrough and allowed crop yields to overcome previous constraints. In the past century agriculture has been characterized by enhanced productivity, the substitution of labour for synthetic fertilizers and pesticides, selective breeding, mechanization, water pollution, and farm subsidies. In recent years there has been a backlash against the external environmental effects of conventional agriculture, resulting in the organic movement.

The changes in the world agriculture can be categorized into four fairly distinct eras, based on how resources were utilized and managed.

Era of Resource Exploitation (before 1900)

Modern agriculture started with the identification and exploitation of production resources. First, prime lands were identified and cleared for farming. The land was tilled and prepared for planting and crop establishment. The basic rationale of this era was that soil productivity was a resource to be exploited for crop productivity. The soil nutrients were repeatedly removed without replacement. This is the mining approach to crop production. This led to the progressive depletion of organic and inorganic soil was deemed unproductive (just like an old mine), it was abandoned for a new fertile site; this was a non-sustainable production approach, requiring new lands to be exploited on a regular basis.

Era of Resource Conservation and Regeneration (early 1900s)

In the early 1900s, producers began adopting production techniques that were less exploitive of the soil. Abandoned farmlands were eventually restored to health, through only after many years in fallow. Crop rotation provided a strategy for a more efficient use of soil moisture that the previous continuous cropping system did not offer. Legumes, through symbiosis, contributed to regeneration of the soil by nitrogen fixation. Organic manure from green manuring (growing a crop for the purpose of ploughing under while still green) and deliberate use of barnyard or livestock manure replenished soil fertility.

Era of Resource Substitution (mid-1900s)

The activities of this era made the industrialization of agriculture possible the period started roughly in the mid-1900s (a little before 1950). This period saw the exploitation of mechanization that has continued to this day. Machines replaced farm draught animals. Supplemental moisture was supplied through crop irrigation. Chemical fertilizers were used more frequently to control weeds and other crop pests. Plant breeders developed more improved cultivars for farms. Technological advances in this era enabled producers to cultivate large tracts of land. The late 1900s saw the introduction of bio-technology and other revolutionary technologies, such as precision farming, into crop production.

Era of Information

Technology will continue to advance. New resources will be discovered. The future of agricultural production will probably be shaped by the producer, as a manager, to translate information and knowledge into value. The use of the internet and other regional and national information networks will continue to make crop production information more readily accessible to producers.

SHARE OF THE AGRIBUSINESS TO RURAL ECONOMY OF ETHIOPIA

Theoretically the role of agriculture in economic development is; agriculture provides both food and raw materials to the rest of the economy; a growing agriculture sector provides an enlarged market as it expands aggregate demand; it also provides labour for employment in the industrial sector; and agriculture is often a principal source of capital for investment elsewhere in the economy. Exports from the agricultural sector are important to earn foreign exchange, which is critical for imports of capital goods and other equipments for rapid industrialization and economic growth.

With this theoretical background, the Ethiopian agricultural sector; on the average accounts for about 49 per cent the country's GDP. From the total foreign exchange earnings about 90 per cent of the exports also goes to the agricultural sector; it also employs about 85 per cent of the labour force; the agricultural sector is also the supplier of foodstuff to consumers and about 70 per cent of raw materials to agro-industries.

In spite of the importance in the national economy, agriculture is largely dependent on subsistence farm household, whose modes of life and work have remained unchanged for centuries. As we have seen the majority of the Ethiopia labour force is employed in agriculture and yet the sector has not been able to satisfy the food requirements of the people. On the other hand the developed countries with a small proportion of their labour force engaged in agriculture, not only have been able to meet the food requirements of their own people, but also feed the hungry elsewhere in the world.

Summary

- **Agribusiness** is a generic term that refers to the various businesses involved in food production, including farming, seed supply, agrichemicals, farm machinery, wholesale and distribution, processing, marketing, and retail sales.
- Agribusiness therefore includes three major sectors — Producers, Agricultural Input firms, and Agricultural Output firms.
- The Ethiopian economy remains heavily dependent on agriculture, which accounts for about 49 per cent of the GDP. An estimated 85 per cent of the population gains its

livelihood directly or indirectly from agricultural production. Coffee export accounts for more than 65 per cent of foreign exchange earnings, while processed and semi-processed hides and skins are the second important foreign exchange earners.

- The rural areas of Ethiopia is determined as inaccessible by transportation means where studies shows that more than 75 per cent of farms are more than half a day walk away from an all weather road. Agricultural inputs and outputs are transported by traditional transport means like pack animals or humans. The poor rural infrastructure affects market efficiency of the rural area. The sale of farm products is confined to the village market specially; perishable agricultural products, which are easily, deteriorate and require quick marketing.
- The Ethiopian agricultural sector; on the average accounts for about 50 per cent of the country's GDP. From the total foreign exchange earnings about 90 per cent of the exports also goes to the agricultural sector; it also employs about 85 per cent of the labour force; the agricultural sector is also the supplier of foodstuff to consumers and about 70 per cent of raw materials to agro-industries.

Self-Learning Activity

Try to answer the following questions on your own:

1. Define agribusiness.
2. Who are the agribusiness producers?
3. Explain the salient features of Ethiopian Economy.
4. What is the share of agribusiness in the Ethiopian Economy?

2

Constraints in Agribusiness

Agribusiness firms have distinctive features as compared to other non-agribusiness firms. Though agribusiness firms include the other non-farm firms such as input supplying firms, processing firms, and marketing and transporting firms, all these are directly dependent on farming and farm products where their supply is determined by the combination of economic, physical and biological factors. There are constraints in agribusiness. They are in terms of: dependence on nature, elasticity of demand and supply and seasonality of agricultural products. These constraints are discussed below in detail.

Highly Dependent on Nature

The following discussion would reveal the constraints as regards to dependence on nature.

The output level of agricultural production is heavily dependent on nature, which affects its supplies. There is a high risk and uncertainty of disease, pests and unfavorable weather condition; basically in developing countries as agriculture is a rain-fed activity it is highly affected by weather condition. The quality and quantity of crops is at the mercy of wind, rain, sun, cold and insects.

So, the intensity, duration and time of rainfall has great impact in agricultural production. Crop and livestock farms face a number of potential natural hazards such as drought, frost, flood, diseases, pest, etc. Unfortunately, these natural hazards are not easily predictable. The farmer can not say definitely how much he will produce, how good the result of his efforts will be, and when the crop will be ready for the market. Thus some year the growing conditions are such that the crop in general is of high quality and more in quantity in other year, unfavorable conditions may result lower quality and lower production. The variation in quality and quantity raises a problem of price fluctuation from time to time due to imbalance in supply and demand; the variation in quality makes it difficult to apply uniform grading standards from year to year; and the variation in quantity throw transportation and storage arrangements out of gear.

Due to this fact agribusiness is the most risky business as compared to other non-agribusiness. Supplies of agricultural outputs are unstable and this will create high risk for food processing and marketing firms. To avoid risk or reduce their uncertainty individual farm operators take different coping mechanisms such as diversification, use of crop insurance, limiting investments, etc.

Inelastic Demand and Supply

Elasticity is a term used to express how responsive the quantity demanded of a product is to a change in the price of that product. Inelastic demand means the percentage change in quantity demands is less than the percentage change in price.

If $e_d < 1$ – inelastic, $e_d = 1$ - unitary elastic, $e_d > 1$ - elastic

Supply elasticity is a measure of how much producers of a product change the quantities they are willing to sell in response to a change in price. If the change in quantity supplied is small relative to a unit change in price, supply is said to be relatively inelastic.

The aggregate agricultural production is not very responsive to price changes. It is mostly assumed that the farmer is less responsive to price changes. In most cases, agriculture tends to use much the same amounts of the factors of production especially land and labor, even when the general level of price is falling. In consequence, the level of total output in agriculture remains remarkably stable from year to year, notwithstanding the fluctuation in the general price level. The most important reason for the insensitivity of the farmer to changes in the relative price of farm commodities in agriculture is a biological process and even if the farmer increases certain acreage of a particular crop or other inputs to increase production in response to price changes, he will not be sure to increase its supply as the total output depends on nature.

In the short-run too aggregate agricultural supply is inelastic, as change to quantity supplied cannot be made quickly to price change. For instance, once a crop is seeded, farmers have limited ability to alter the quantities they put on the market.

It is proved by many studies that demand elasticity of major agricultural products are inelastic which make agriculture a very risky business. The main reason for this is that as agriculture is mainly production of foodstuffs which is necessary for life, thus peoples need is limited, as a result the demand for all agricultural products taken together tends to be inelastic. When prices of agricultural goods fall, consumption not greatly expands, nor will it greatly contract if food price rise. In any given year a farmer has to sink a fairly large fixed cost into planting, tending and harvesting, but his revenues are highly dependent on the weather. If the weather is especially good everywhere, there will be a bumper crops, sales volume will be high but price will be low and, because crop demand is inelastic revenues will also be low. On the other hand when the weather is generally bad overall supply will be low and price will be high. If a particular farmer is fortunate in that bad year that farmer's revenue will be much higher than during a good year because demand is inelastic. The unlucky farmer will receive no revenue and pay high fixed costs.

The implication is that when there is high production the price will fall dramatically and decreases the revenues. On the other hand, when there is low production the price will rise and total revenue of the firm will increase.

Agricultural products are also income inelastic as compared to other type of goods and services. Income elasticity demand is the increase in expenditure on commodity when there is an increase in income per capita, other things remaining the same. A one per cent change in income of consumers will result in a less than one per cent in expenditure in agricultural products, other things being equal. When people improve their standard of living, they substitute better food for their plain fare. But beyond a certain point, when their income increases, people start spending more on non-agricultural goods. Hence, even if there is a general increase in the per capita income, there will be relatively small increase in the per capita demand for food.

Large Number of Independent Producers

Geographic scatter and the absence of pronounced technical or internal economies of large scale particularly in the crops economy accounts for large number of farm firms, the world over. They are family concerns employing little hired labor and produce for their own consumption. It is proved by many studies that more than 85 per cent of Ethiopian population is engaged in agriculture. Farmers are small with fragmented land scattered over large place with poor infrastructure and most of them are illiterate that strive to fulfill their food requirement. Thus, most agricultural firms other than farming business such as input supplying, processing and marketing are also affected, as they are dependent on the farming sector.

Seasonality of Agricultural Products

The seasonality of agricultural products also has an impact in the operation of agribusiness. Agricultural products grow in different seasons where there is favorable weather condition— sunshine, rain, temperature, and wind — in the year and the life process of plants and animals which depends in the biological rhythm of nature, reinforcing that of the seasons, which leave the farmer little control over the time cycle of the tempo of production. Thus they are ready for market in certain fixed period of the year only. Thus, there is no constant supply of farm products to market; at certain periods of the year there is superfluity of supply and at the other periods a dearth.

Agribusinesses are likely to be affected by the seasonal nature of agricultural products. The main problems that may arise due to seasonality can be; labor shortage during peak periods and excess labor during slack period's and excess supply right after harvest and shortage other times. To the extent the commodity can be stored, the facilities must be provided to hold the product, but in peak season the stores will be used at near capacity and at other times, they may be almost empty. If the product cannot be stored, it must either be processed or consumed immediately. Due to seasonal production, the processing plants will be running at full capacity for some periods and well below capacity for other periods. In case the product must move directly into consumption transportation and refrigeration facilities must be immediately available. All of these special situations mean increased costs in the agricultural marketing process.

Agricultural products are bulkier and more perishable

Compared to most other products agricultural products are both bulkier and perishable. When things are bulky marketing functions with their physical handling are very much affected. In case of those products which occupy a lot of space in relation to their value, the unit cost of transportation and storage is automatically raised. Similarly many agricultural products are exceedingly perishable. Even though the degree of perishability varies from product to product; perishability is a distinct characteristic of agricultural products. These characteristics have their effect on the facilities necessary for to market farm products. Their bulkiness necessitates large storage and higher cost of transportation. Perishable products require speedy handling as well as special refrigeration. Due to these characteristics, agricultural marketing sometimes is costlier than marketing of industrial products.

Agricultural investments are mostly parked-up capital

Once investment is done, it is not possible to change into another type of business or to shift to another place where it can be more profitable. For instance once irrigation scheme is constructed, it is not possible to move this investment to another place or to change the capital into another type of business. This would increase the risk and would also force the business to run even at loss.

Table 2.1: Examples of Production Agriculture (Kinds of Farms)

Farms Producing Animals and/or Animal Products	Major Product Produced
• Beef cattle farms/ranches	• Meat (beef)
• Swine farms	• Meat (pork)
• Sheep farms	• Meat (lamb and mutton), wool
• Poultry farms	• Meat (chicken, turkey, etc.), eggs
• Dairy farms	• Milk, butter, cheese
• Horse farms	• Recreation and work horses
• Fish farms	• Food and recreation
Farms Producing Plants and/or Plant Products	**Major Product Produced**
• Vegetable farms	• Vegetables (beans, tomatoes, potatoes, broccoli, etc.)
• Cash grain farms	• Corn, wheat, rice, soybean, etc.
• Cotton farms	• Cotton (fibre for clothing) and seed (oil and animal feed)
• Tobacco farms	• Tobaccoo
• Fruit farms	• Fruit (apple, citrus, peaches, etc.)
• Tree farms	• Timber: Saw logs (for lumber), pulpwood (for paper and similar products)

Table 2.2: Examples of supplies and services required in production agriculture

Supplies Required in Production of Agriculture		Services Required in Production of Agriculture	
For Farmers	*For Ranchers*	*For Farmers*	*For Ranchers*
CREDIT • Long Term • Intermediate Term • Long Term	VETERINARY SUPPLIES • Biological • Syringes • Dehorners • Wormers	• Ploughing • Planting • Spraying • Fertilizing • Harvesting • Drying • Shearing sheet • Leveling land • Constructing water facilities (ponds, drainage, ditches (etc.) • Grinding feed • Mixing feed • Treating feed • Buying to order (cattle order buyers etc.) • Drilling water wells	• Vaccinating • Spraying • Inspecting • Dehorning • Treating injuries • Horseshoe fitting
MACHINERY • Tractors • Planters • Sprayers • Harrows • Ploughs • Harvestors • Irrigation equipment • Spare parts	FUEL AND OIL • Gasoline • Diesel Fuel • Motor oil • Hydraulic fluid • Lubricating grease		

FEED • Concentrates • Vitamins • Minerals	CHEMICALS • Herbicides • Insecticides • Fungicides • Fumigants • Defoliants
HAND TOOLS • Hammers • Wrenches • Hoes • Shovels	FERTILIZER • Liquid • Solid • Gaseous • Slurries
MATERIALS • Lumber • Roofing Materials • Fencing wire • Paint • Nails • Bolts • Screws • Pipe	SEED • Vegetables • Ornamentals • Agronomic
	OTHER • Fruit trees • Berry plants
	ELECTRICAL POWER

NATURE OF DEMAND OF AGRICULTURAL PRODUCTS

Concept of Market Forces

The key function of markets is to determine the price of the products at which the product should change hands. This process goes on continually at all times and places between buyers and sellers. Price determination is a process of balancing demand with supply in a capitalistic economic order; price system is an important means of allocating society's scarce resources among alternative uses. The phenomenon of pricing is a reflection of scarcity of goods and services in relation to their demand. In a competitive economic system, pricing performs three most important functions.

Firstly it directs the consumption of products and services. It helps a consumer in deciding what to buy and how much to spend on each product taking into account the relative prices of the products and services and the amount of satisfaction expected to be derived from them. Secondly, it also directs the use of resources in production. It helps the farmer-producer in deciding what to produce how to produce and how much to produce. These decisions are based on relative prices of products and inputs, along with information on physical input-output relationships. Thirdly, it helps to distribute income among the owner of productive agents. Price variations result in the redistribution of incomes and property values among owners of productive agents. Thus, we find that the knowledge of pricing is of vital to the farmer producer.

The forces which affect the process of price determination, either directly or indirectly may be termed as 'market forces'. The forces may be tangible, like the quantity and arrival at a particular point of time in the market or heavy rainfall; or intangible like the announcement of government policy. All these factors affect the price determination by affecting either the demand behaviour of the buyers or the supply behaviour of the sellers.

Supply and demand is the two fundamental components of a market. Supply describes how producers or manufacturers, large or small, react or behave in the market place in producing and selling a product. On the other hand demands of consumer are usually considered to be the prime force in determining what is produced and how much is produced. The economic concept of demand relates to the choices consumers make in purchasing a product.

Concept of Demand

Demand for a particular product or service represents the quantity people are willing to purchase at various prices at any given time or during a given period of time. Utility, that is the want satisfying quality of goods and services, is the prime factor that generates demand. In theory a product is said to be having demand when it is backed by the ability to buy, the desire to buy and the willingness to buy. Demand is a relationship between price and quantity, with all other factors remaining constant. The law of demand says "other things being constant, when the price of a commodity increases, the quantity demanded of the product decreases and vice versa". That is there is an inverse relationship between price and quantity. In other words, the higher the price the lower the quantity demanded and, conversely, the lower the price the higher the quantity desired. Demand is represented graphically as a downward sloping curve.

Table 2.3: Demand schedule of apple at a given time and place at different price levels

Amount buyers stand to buy	Price of apple (in birr)/Kg
10	5
9	6
8	7
7	8
6	9
5	10

Diagram 2.1

(a) *Individual and market demand*

The concept of demand applies to a single individual or firm as well as to any number of buyers in a market. The transition from an individual to a market demand schedule is accomplished by summing the quantities demanded by each buyer at the various possible prices.

For example, corn like most products has many uses; the total market demand is the sum of the demands for each of these uses by all buyers and users whether the corn moves through a specific market or not. The market demand curve is the sum of all the individual demand curves. The market demand is composed of the aggregate purchases of corn by all buyers.

(b) *Direct and indirect demand*

Demand for goods that are directly used for consumption by the ultimate consumer is known as *direct demand*. Since such goods are used for final consumption, such demand is also called *consumer's good demand*. Demand for all consumers good's such as bread, tea, houses is direct demand. Indirect demand is the demand for goods that are not used by consumers directly. They are used by producers for producing other goods. So, indirect demand is also known as *producer's goods demand*. Examples of indirect demand are demands for machines, coals, limestone and raw materials. However the distinction between direct and indirect demand is subjective. When the demand for wheat comes from a consumer for his personal use it is direct demand while when it comes from a spaghetti manufacturer it is indirect demand. The determinants of these types of demand are different.

This categorization is helpful in proper analysis of demand. While direct demand depends primarily on the consumer demand, indirect demand depends on the concerned producer's output. In the above example, if demand for wheat depends on consumer income while demand for wheat by the manufacturer depends on the demand for the processed food spaghetti.

(c) *Derived and Autonomous demand*

The classification of demand as derived and autonomous is quite similar to its classification as direct and indirect. When a product derives its usage from the use of some primary product, its demand is known as *derived demand.* For example, the demand for fertilizers and seeds are not having direct demand. They are not demanded for their own sake. They are demanded because; the use of them in the production of crops will increase the yields. So the demand for some commodities exists only because they are used in producing other commodities, which are directly demanded by consumers. *Autonomous demand* is the demand for a product that can be independently used. Thus, while the demand for agricultural inputs like fertilizer is derived since their demand depends on the demand on farm products the demand for milk or vegetables is autonomous. However, since almost all products depend on others to some extent, the difference between the two is of more degree.

(d) *Reservation demand and price*

Reservation demand denotes that a certain quantity of the products will be retained by the sellers at a given price. At different prices, the seller himself has a demand to keep a certain quantity with himself, for selling later.

The seller may not sell his produce at one price, for the actual price is lower than his expected price for his product. The pre-conceived price is termed as remunerative price. At any point of time, a schedule showing the quantity to be retained or, the quantity to be sold at each price may be developed for each stockiest. Such a schedule may be termed as remunerative demand and price schedule.

(e) *Shift in Demand*

A demand shifts occurs when consumers are willing to buy different quantities of a product at all price levels. The movement in the demand curve is referred to as a shift outward of demand or as a shift to the right when consumers are willing to buy more of a product at all price levels. The movement is referred to as a shift inward or as a shift of demand to the left.

Shifts in demand occur from changes unrelated to product's own price. The market demand for a commodity shifts over time as a result of changes in population, income, consumer preferences and the price of related goods.

Usually, shifts in demand for agricultural commodities occur slowly and, therefore, are reasonably predictable. This is because the major determinants of demand such as population and income change gradually rather than suddenly. There are, however, some exceptions to this general rule. Circumstances such as health care can also have an abrupt and discernible affect on demand.

All the above concepts on demand can be applied in agribusiness. The demand for agricultural products is in line with these different concepts of demand. Circumstances and situations in market place lead to the applications of the demand for agricultural products in the market. These demand situations explain the nature of demand for agricultural products.

Factors Affecting Demand of the Farm Products

Market demand for an agricultural commodity is usually derived from demand for a finished product. For example, a family's demand for bread creates farm gate demand for wheat. A number of factors help to determine how much a consumer will buy.

The following are some of the most important factors affecting demand for the farm products.

Income

As income limits what a person can buy when there is a higher income consumers want to use higher quality products which affects the demand for a specific commodity. The relation between changes in income and changes in demand are somewhat more complex. An increase in income will increase the demand for most agricultural products. Consumers typically buy more meat and other animal products as their income increases. Goods or commodities, whose demand varies directly with money income are called normal or superior goods. Economic progress in currently developing countries will greatly increase the demand for such products.

Although most products including farm food products are normal goods, there are some exceptions. Economic studies generally reveal that as incomes increases beyond some point, the amount of cereals, or baking products, purchased at each price does not increase. The higher incomes permit consumer to buy more of the prepared bakery products and of greater importance more high protein meats, poultry, fish and dairy products. In addition, rising incomes tends to cause the demand for cheaper cuts of meat to decline as consumers switch preferences to higher priced steacks, prime ribs and the like. Goods whose demand varies inversely with a change in money income are sometimes called inferior goods.

The relationship between income and quantity purchased is measured by a coefficient called income elasticity of demand. A number of studies have revealed that income elasticity in relation to total food is very low and it is generally lower among people with high incomes than among people with low income. This is as results of most of agricultural products are necessities of life and their demand is limited to some level by the extent of human stomach. Where peoples purchase shift to a better quality agricultural product than increasing the quantity of purchase for specific food as their income increase.

Price of a commodity

This is always important; household's demand for an agricultural commodity is influenced by the price of that commodity. Usually the higher the price, the lower the quantity purchased. This is because there are substitutes for most commodities.

Price of related goods

Whether the demand for a given product will be increased or decreased by a change in the price of a related product depends on whether the latter is a substitute for, or a complement to, the product under consideration. Tea and coffee, for example, are competing or substitute products. When the price of tea rises, consumers will purchase less tea and this will cause the demand for coffee to increase. Similarly as the price of tea falls the demand for coffee decreases. When two products are substitutes, a change in the price is directly related to the demand for the other. This is the case with tea and coffee, oranges and grapefruit and so on.

When two products are used together such as bread and butter, milk and cereal they are complements. A rise in the price of one will decrease the demand for the other, and vice versa. Two products are complements if an inverse relationship exists between the price of one the demand for the other.

When two products are not related at all in terms of price and quantity demanded, they are said to be independent. The relationship between some food and non-food products sometimes fall in this category. We should expect the price of one to have little effect on the demand for the other.

Religious teachings

Many Hindus do not eat beef, and some of them are completely vegetarian. Muslims and Jews do not eat pig meat. Christians do not eat meat and milk products at the time of fasting which affects the demand for these particular products and the demand for non meat and milk products. All affect the demand for agricultural products.

Traditional prohibitions

This is mostly the case of developing countries where norms cultures dominate the societies living style. Some groups in Africa will not eat eggs and poultry.

Habits

A household demand for agricultural products is also influenced by the cultures and habits prevailing in the society. People enjoy the food they are used to. Our liking for certain foods depends on the food our parents gave us when we are children; the types of food which are available locally; the family's social status; the cultural, background etc.

Tastes and preferences

A change in consumers' tastes favorable to a product will mean that more is demanded at each price, or the demand increases. An unfavorable change in consumer's tastes will cause the demand to decrease. Consumers prefer to use products with a good taste if they afford it. For instance, many people prefer to use white teff than red teff if the price is low.

NATURE OF THE SUPPLY OF AGRICULTURAL PRODUCTS

Concept of Supply

Supply describes how producers react in the market place. By the supply of a commodity we mean the amount of that commodity producers are able and willing to offer for sale at a given price. Supply may be carefully distinguished from stock and production. Stock constitutes the potential supply but supply at a time is that part of the stock which is offered for sale in the market. The product of the total produce which the farmer is willing to sell is the stock and is known as marketable surplus and the portion which is actually brought to the market at a particular time for sale is the supply of the produce and is labeled at marketed surplus. Similarly supply is to be distinguished from total production. A farmer may keep back a part of his total output for his own consumption. Similarly supply of the farm produce, sometimes, may be more than the current production if past stocks are also brought to the market along with it.

There is a direct relationship between the supply and the price. When the price of a commodity is higher the lager will be the quantity that is offered for sale and vice versa. The law of supply says that when the price increases, other things remaining constant, the supply also increases and vice versa. Like the demand schedule, here also there is supply schedule and the supply curve. A price rise benefits the producer because, the difference between the cost per unit of the product and the returns from each unit will be greater and so his total revenue goes up. This however, is true only in the short period when the supply is fixed. But in the long run if the increased price continues, producers will increase their scale of production. So, the supply will increase normally if the price of the commodity rises.

Table 2.4: A hypothetical supply schedule for the apples in the market

Price of apple (per Kg)	Supply (in thousands)
5	50
6	150
7	300
9	350
12	400
15	450
20	500

The supply curve based on the supply schedule will have an upward slopping curve as shown in the Diagram 2.2. The curve rises upward as the price of apples goes up steadily.

Market supply or aggregate supply represents the amount of a product all producers are willing to sell over a range of prices at any given time period. Market supply is represented graphically as an upward sloping curve. That is the relationship between price and supply is positive.

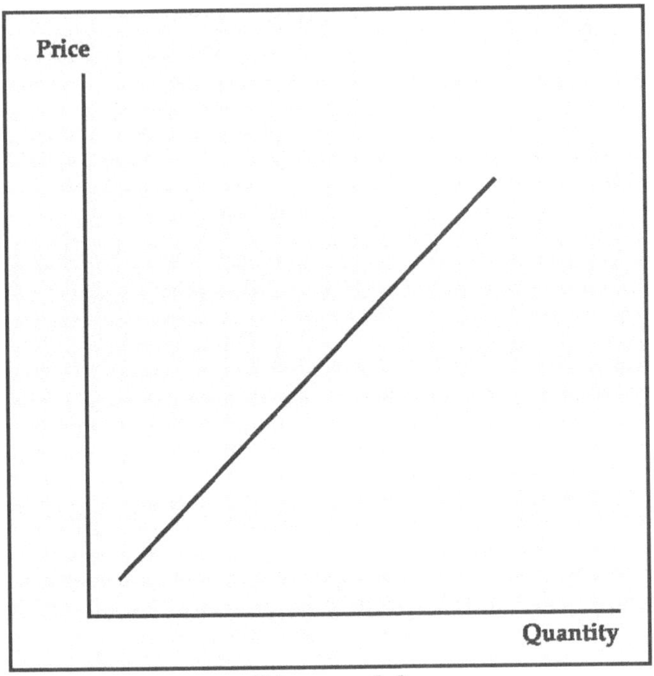

Diagram 2.2

Time is very important factor in the supply analysis. The given supply exists at a given time. The time periods are of different types.

1. *Short run:* The short period is one during which fixed cost cannot be changed, only the variable can be changed. So, in the short period, only to some extent, the supply can be increased, when there is increase in demand.
2. *Intermediate run:* This refers to the time during which commodities can be produced only with the existing production facilities. The existing capacity puts an upper limit on the quantity that can be offered for sale.
3. *Long run:* Long period is one where both the cost i.e., both the fixed costs can be changed so that all the increase in demand can be fully met. In the long run, supply is more responsive to prices and other incentives.

The time element greatly complicates the process of the supply of agricultural product.

Shifts in Supply

A supply shift is a change in market supply at all price levels. Shifts in supply occur as a result of change of factors that are not related with the price of the product itself. A shift outward in supply curve occurs when producers are willing to produce more of a product at all price levels.

The number of firms producing a product affects supply in the same way as the number of consumers (size of population) affects demand: the more firms producing, the greater and more competitive the supply. The opposite also applies — fewer firms generally produce a smaller supply. Of course, the size of producers is not strictly the number of firms or farms, but also the size of those farms. If the number of farms decline, but with increased size of farm land the supply increases.

The adoption of technology in agriculture has expanded agricultural output. The price of inputs can also change the supply, if input price raises a smaller amount product produced without the producer paying higher on costs. If the price of fertilizer increases, either less fertilizer is used or total expenditure on inputs must be increased.

The price of substitute products changes, producers may switch their production decisions. For example, if the price of barely is expected to go up relative to the price of wheat, producers may alter their cropping patterns to produce more barely and less wheat. When all production inputs have been committed, there are still important random influences on supply such as weather, insects that are impossible to forecast.

Shift in supply graphically can be represented as an outward movement of the supply curve or the movement of the supply curve to the right which shows an increase in supply. The decrease in supply can be represented by inward moving supply curve or the movement of the supply curve to the left.

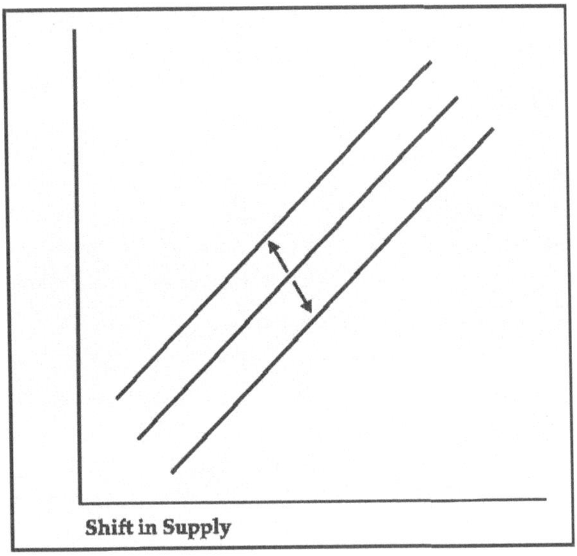

Diagram 2.3

Factors Determining the Supply of Agricultural Product

There are several factors that affect the supply of agricultural products. They are: price of the products, number of firms producing the product, technology advancements, price of inputs, price of other products, expectations about prices and unpredictable situations. Each of these factors are discussed hereunder.

Price of the product

Supply of agricultural commodities is affected by the price that commodity commands in the market. Other things remaining the same, the higher the price of the commodity the more profitable will be to increase its supply.

Number of firms producing the product

Given the scale of operation of each firm, the larger the number of producers, the greater will be the market supply. As more producers enter an industry, the supply curve will shift to the right. Conversely, the smaller the number of producers, the smaller the market supply.

Technology advances

Supply of goods also depends on the state of technology. The agricultural technology helps in bringing down the cost of production and hence increases the supply.

Price of inputs

The supply of agricultural commodities would depend upon its cost of production that is the prices of factors of production which are involved in the production of a given commodity. For example, a rise in the price of fertilizers, seeds etc. will increase the cost of production of the farm products thus leading to a decrease in the supply of these products as farmers decrease the use of these inputs. Conversely a fall in the price of the inputs may lead to increase in the supply.

Price of other products

Changes in the prices of other products that can be substituted in production may change the supply of a given product. An increase in the prices of other commodities will make the production of the commodity whose price has not risen relatively less attractive to the producers than it was previously.

This mainly leads to changes in cropping pattern in agriculture. An increase in the price of soybeans, for example, may cause a farmer to shift some land from corn to soybeans, thus reducing the supply of corn. Conversely, a decrease in the price of soybeans, with other things remaining the same, will tend to increase the supply of corn.

Expectations about prices

Expectations about price of a product may affect the current supply. Here, however, it is difficult to generalize. The expectation of a higher price of corn may induce farmers to withhold some of their current harvest from market, thus reducing the current supply of the day or week. Conversely, the expectation of a higher price may cause farmers to plant more corn, and in anticipation of a large crop they may reduce the amount corn held in storage, thus increasing the current supply of the day or week.

Unpredictable events such as the weather

Weather, in particular, rainfall is a significant factor in supply response of farmers. In the wake of the uncertain rains, farmers will prefer to sow low income yielding crops if these are drought resistant. On the other hand, farmers who receive assured water supply can enjoy greater freedom in planning production in response to price changes. It is also common in developing countries under unfavorable weather conditions farmers will not harvest what they sow thus in general leading to a decrease in supply while at the time of favorable weather conditions their harvest will be high and the supply also increases.

Summary

- Markets help to determine the price of the products at which the product should change hands. Supply and demand is the two fundamental components of a market. Supply describes how producers or manufacturers, large or small, react or behave in the market place in producing and selling a product.
- On the other hand demands of consumer are usually considered to be the prime force in determining what is produced and how much is produced. The economic concept of demand relates to the choices consumers make in purchasing a product. The law of demand says "other things being constant, when the price of a commodity increases, the quantity demanded of the product decreases and vice versa".
- Demand for agricultural products can be affected by income, price of a commodity, price of related goods, religious teachings, traditional prohibitions, habits, and tastes and preferences. Shifts in demand occur from

changes unrelated to product's own price which is graphically represented by an inward or outward movement of the demand curve. Like shift in demand shifts in supply occur as a result of change of factors that are not related with the price of the product itself.

- The supply of agricultural products can be determined by price of the product, the number of firms producing the product, technology advances, price of inputs, price of other products, expectation about prices, unpredictable conditions such as weather.

Self-Learning Activity

Try to answer the following questions on your own:

1. How far the dependence of nature acts as a constraint to agribusiness?
2. Explain perishable nature of agricultural products?
3. Give an account of market forces in agriculture.
4. What do you mean by shift in supply?

3

Infrastructure in Agribusiness

Introduction

The word infrastructure has originated as a military term during the World War II applied to such items as oil pipelines. Subsequently, after World War II, the term was generally used as a substitute for the 'social overhead capital' with a view to avoid confusion with hospitals, schools and similar other welfare type facilities. The word infrastructure has also been defined as the basic services on public utilities, which are necessary to commodity producing sectors of the economy.

Infrastructure and superstructure are both complementary parts of a single structure. Infrastructure comprises all those facilities and activities, which provide sustenance to income generation and production within the infrastructure enterprises themselves.

Infrastructure can be divided into economic and social, the former comprising services such as power, irrigation, transport, communication, banking, insurance, etc. and the latter consisting of services and amenities like water supply, sewerage, education, medical and health services, housing, etc.

Definition of Infrastructure

Infrastructures are usually defined as the underlying basic buildings, institutions and facilities or other essential elements that are necessary to sustain and enable growth and development of a community.

The concept of infrastructure originally stems from the military as mentioned earlier. According to the definition of NATO — infrastructure is a term generally applicable to all fixed and permanent installations, fabrications, or facilities for the support and control of military forces (DOD Military terms 1999). In the civilian world the concept of infrastructure was adapted, but lost some of its content.

The word "infrastructure" has been defined in many of the following ways:

In *Merriam Webster Dictionary* one of the definitions of infrastructure is the resources (as personnel, buildings, or equipment) required for an activity. According to Larimer (1994) infrastructure refers to the foundation or underlying framework of basic services, facilities and institutions upon which the growth and development of an area, community or a system depend. Infrastructure, therefore, includes a broad spectrum of services, institutions and facilities that ranges from transportation systems and public utilities to finance systems, laws and law enforcement, and education and research.

The Lexical Database for English Cognitive Science Laboratory (Word Net (r) 1.6a), for example, provides two definitions of infrastructure:

(i) the basic framework or features of a system or organization; and

(ii) the basic facilities and equipment needed for the functioning of a country or area; think of "the industrial base of Japan". Therefore, a synonym for infrastructure in this respect could be "base".

The definition of Infrastructure found in the *Wordsmyth English Dictionary* — Thesaurus is: the basic facilities and equipment, especially of a technological nature, that are necessary for a system or organization to function.

Weijnen and Bosgra (1999) define infrastructure as the basic facilities, equipment, and installations needed to provide the utility products and services crucial for the growth and functioning of an economy, community or organization. The collection of basic facilities, equipment, and installations refers both to the hardware of the infrastructure (needed to fulfill the basic transport, distribution, storage and processing functions of the infrastructure) and to the safety and control engineering systems (not only hardware devices, but including operational procedures, organization and management) needed to make the system function according to its functional specifications. The first and foremost functional specification of a physical infrastructure is that the system is able to match supply and demand of the utility product and/or services, on a range of time scales:

(i) the evolutionary time scale, i.e. a time scale varying between decades and years, depending on the type of infrastructure and the rate of system innovation.

(ii) a range of operational time scales, with respect to e.g., seasonal and daily demand fluctuations.

The *Merriam Webster Dictionary* gives the following definitions for infrastructure:

(i) the underlying foundation or basic framework (as of a system or organization);

(ii) the permanent installations required for military purposes; and

(iii) the system of public works of a country, state, or region.

It may be seen that the waste management sector falls into the category of public works that, apart from waste management, includes electric power, natural gas and water systems. These public infrastructures are based on a specific type of physical infrastructure to provide the goods or services. The fourth definition of infrastructure found in *Merriam Webster Dictionary* is:

(iv) the resources (as personnel, buildings, or equipment) required for an activity.

As the term infrastructure has diverse meaning in different fields *economically* it could be seen to be the structural elements of an economy which allow for production of goods and services without themselves being part of the production process. E.g. roads allow the transport of raw materials and finished products.

The concept of infrastructure, is not unambiguous, many definitions of infrastructure exists. It is clear from the above definitions that infrastructures play key roles in our society. The many definitions throughout the literature show common features of infrastructure, such as:

- Infrastructure is a large-scale system,
- Infrastructure has a strong technological dimension,
- Infrastructure consists of immovable physical components,
- Infrastructure delivers an essential services.

Using these features, the following workable definition of infrastructure was derived — an infrastructure is a large-scale technological system, consisting of immovable physical facilities and delivering an essential public or private service(s) through the storage, conversion and/or transportation of certain commodities. The infrastructure includes those parts and subsystems necessary for fulfilling the primary storage, transportation, and/or conversion function as well as those supporting proper executions of these functions.

The infrastructure includes very many facilities in agribusiness is very much important. The infrastructure facilities are the systems, which support the agricultural sector to transport agricultural produces and products from one place to another or to the marketplace for sales and distribution. Communication is very important facility to communicate information on price, place, and other market information to the needy people who are engaged themselves in agribusiness. In agribusiness storage and warehousing are the major required facilities. The government, non-governmental agencies, and cooperatives are making arrangement to store and preserve the agribusiness. These various infrastructure facilities are discussed in a detailed manner in transport and communication and storage and warehousing sections of this unit.

Market Infrastructure

Infrastructure is a key factor for performance and for improving the efficiency of any system. Marketing infrastructure involves physical and institutional infrastructure. Further; physical market infrastructure can be put under two categories:

(a) directly related to marketing; and

(b) indirectly related to marketing.

The first category includes, the network of market, and facilities for storage, processing and grading. The second category includes rural roads, transportation facilities and communication facilities. These are not directly involved in marketing and improving its efficiency.

Physical infrastructure alone is not adequate to improve the market performance. It has to be supported by appropriate institutional infrastructure to meet desired goals from agricultural marketing system.

Physical Infrastructure

The foremost marketing infrastructure is the network of a well established and regulated market. Proper storage is necessary to maintain quality and to reduce losses. Proper storage provides protection against losses from moisture ingress, insect-pest infestation and damage by the rodents.

Road connectivity plays a crucial role in connecting the production points with market and through speedy and efficient movement of produce.

Institutional Infrastructure

Physical infrastructure alone is not adequate to improve the marketing performance. It has to be supported by appropriate institutional infrastructure to meet the desired goals from agricultural marketing system. As private trade in developing countries like Ethiopia is underdeveloped and not equipped to meet the needs of growing economy, the government set up several public-sector institutions and cooperative marketing organizations to improve the market structure, conduct and perform and to help growers in marketing and realization better returns for their produce.

Infrastructure Necessary for Agribusiness

Although the important items of infrastructure remain the same, the diverse requirements of marketing of agricultural produce may call for a quite different infrastructure than that of the needs of other spheres.

There are some necessary infrastructure facilities for agribusiness. Such important items of infrastructure for the growth of marketing of agricultural produce are as follows:

- Processing
- Transportation
- Wholesale assembly
- Godown/storage/cold storage facility and warehousing
- Roads
- Regulated agricultural markets besides rural market
- Marketing finance
- Other agencies for disposal and procurement (like regulated markets/cooperative marketing/commodity corporations/state agencies, etc).

Infrastructures are largely responsible for increase in marketing efficiency. In the agricultural sector agricultural output comes from small farms which require some forms of infrastructures to efficiently assemble, process and distribution to consumers in the same way the supply of improved seeds fertilizers and pesticides to the farmer.

The distinct nature of agricultural products makes transportation and communication, storages and warehouses to be the necessary infrastructure for agribusiness. Since most farms are far from major cities where consumers found it necessary to have transportation systems. Deficit of communication and transportation limits the range of marketing where the sale of agricultural produces to be confined to nearby consumers and farmers are not able to have market information to sell their products at proper prices. Many agricultural producers are still confined to village market, and will remain so until appropriate transport facilities make other outlets accessible.

Inadequacy of the other facilities in the agribusiness storage and warehousing facilities also cause heavy losses of agricultural produce in many parts of the world. These result in a serious wastage of foodstuffs and increased costs to consumer. The hot, humid conditions of many parts of the tropics are especially favorable to insect infestation and mould growth in grain and to rapid decomposition of more perishable products. In order to avoid losses and quality deterioration many farmers are obliged to sell their produce as soon as it is harvested. This results farmers to sell their product in very low prices because of the high supply at harvest and farmers lack bargaining power.

TRANSPORT AND COMMUNICATION

TRANSPORTATION

Transportation is a necessary function of marketing because most of the markets are geographically separated from the areas of production Majority of manufacturing plants and farms are far away from their most important markets and major cities because of various factors. All goods whether agricultural or manufactured are not utilized at the place of their origin, they require some kind of transportation to create place of utility.

Meaning of Transportation

Transportation is shipping materials to required places or getting materials to where they are required. Transportation can be freight transportation or passenger transportation. Freight transportation is shipping of products to the required place or getting materials to where they are required whereas passenger transportation is transporting of peoples.

Advantages of Transportation

Transportation has a large number of advantages. But we consider here some of its contribution to agribusiness with particular reference to marketing.

- It helps in the growth of industries whose products require quick marketing. For instance, articles like fish, vegetables and flower are carried to various consumers quickly even in distant market.
- Through transportation of products to new places, newer customers can be easily contacted and supplied. This widens the market. It increases the demand for goods.
- By virtue of improvements in the speed of transport, it offers timely utility to products.
- It helps to stabilize prices of several commodities. This is achieved by moving commodities from surplus areas to deficit areas. This will equalize the supply and demand factors and make the price of commodities to even out.
- It ensures even flow of commodities into the hands of consumers since it increases marketing efficiency linking the different marketing activities. For instance, without transportation links, raw materials can not flow into the warehouses and plants, nor can the finished products flow out of the plant to field warehouse and finally to the consumer.

- It enables the consumers to enjoy the benefits of many goods not produced locally. This increases the standard of living, an essential factor for further development of marketing and the economy.
- Transport intensifies competition, which in turn, reduces prices; prices are also reduced because of the facilities offered by transport for large-scale production.

Modes of Transportation

There are five major modes of transportation: airlines, motor carriers, pipelines, railroads and water carriers. Each of these modes has distinct characteristics that give them advantage over the others. Which method is best depends on the following:

- *Freight hauled:* The type of product to be transported whether it is perishable or not, and whether it is bulk or not.
- *Cost:* The charge for transporting the product in that mode.
- *Speed:* The time taken to deliver the product to its destination using the mode.
- *Reliability:* How much the product will arrive safely to its destination using a given mode of transportation.
- *Capability:* The availability of the transportation mode.
- *Capacity:* The amount the transportation mode is able to haul in one delivery.
- *Length of haul:* Whether the product is transported for longer distance or short distance.
- *Flexibility:* The ability of the transportation mode to provide door-to-door service.

Airlines

Airlines are the fastest mode of transportation. This is their primary advantage. They specialize in the transportation of time sensitive movement of documents, perishable items, technical instruments, medical supplies, and high valued products. For light weight and perishable commodities with high value, the contribution of air transport is significant. Today flowers and fruits can be provided to international markets through Airlines. Airfreight services cost more than other modes. They provide terminal to terminal service, meaning direct delivery to a consumer's door is the rarest of exceptions. Airlines are reasonably reliable. While weather-related flight delays might disrupt service, the disrupted service is often still faster than the next fastest mode. Airlines transport small volume shipments rather than large volumes, and packaged products rather than heavy, bulk commodities.

Motor carriers

Motor carriers are the most flexible major mode of transportation. It may go near to the place of loading and deliver the goods at the place of use. This means better direct access to motor carriage for more shippers and final consumers. This door-to-door service is their most attractive feature. Motor carriers also have the advantage of broad geographic coverage. Because trailers vary in length, temperature control, and form, motor carriers can carry a variety of products.

Motor carriers are susceptible to delays because of bad weather or traffic congestion and also they are not well suited to handle extremely heavy, bulk products. Most agricultural products and supplies are transported by truck from farms or ranches to processing plants and consumers.

Pipelines

Pipelines are a unique mode of transportation which is fixed in place, and the product moves through them. This limits the types of products they can transport. They can transport material only in a liquid or gaseous state such as oil, natural gas and crude oil. Pipelines, which move solid materials such as coal that is suspended in a liquid, also exist.

Railroads

Railroads haul high density, low-valued freight over long distances at rates lower than trucking and air. Products hauled include coal, stone, sand, metals, grain and automobiles. They lack flexibility, that is they cannot offer door-to-door services. Goods have to be transported to terminals (railway stations) causing additional transport and loading charges.

Recently, rail is regaining some freight lost to motor carriers through increase in inter-modal operations; a transportation method of using more than one mode of transportation to move goods from origin to destination. In the inter-modal operation of rail cars standardize containers that can be removed from a ship are placed directly on a rail car for surface transportation. This will avoid loading and unloading charges. Inter-modal transportation allows shippers to compromise on the benefit of each mode used to transport the product.

Water carriers

Water carriers dominate international transportation because of their cost-structure and ability to transport large volumes. Advantages of water transport include long-haul capabilities, particularly for low valued products such as coal, stone, grain, and ores at low rates. They can and do haul broad range of products. Since water carriers haul a wide variety of commodities, they operate a variety of ships. Tankers primarily carry liquid products like petroleum and crude oil. Bulk carriers are constructed to haul commodities like coal, iron ore, or agricultural products. Furthermore, significant growth in container ships where standardized containers are loaded placed on and shipped across the ocean to their destination.

Water carriers are relatively slow, unreliable, and inflexible compared with other modes. They depend on other modes for door-to-door delivery and suffer from a high degree of variability in delivery schedules. The initial cost of the ship is significant, but the volume transported over the useful life of the ship is so large that the cost per unit is relatively low.

TRANSPORTING AGRICULTURAL PRODUCTS

Most of agricultural products and supplies are transported by truck, rail or water. Air transportation is not commonly used except for certain specialized products and supplies which are highly perishable. Products such as flowers and fish are shipped frequently by air.

Since many farm products, especially food, are delicate as well as perishable they must be moved carefully as well as quickly. Delays in getting highly perishables to the processors result in spoilage, making the products worthless.

The following are some of the examples for taking care while transporting agricultural products:

- Cut flowers must be delivered quickly and carefully by air freight at long distances or by motor trucks at short distances. They must arrive undamaged, looking fresh and appealing enough for customers who want to buy them.
- If fertilizer comes in bags, they must be handled so that they do not get wet or burst open.
- Cattle must be moved carefully from the farm or ranch to buyers so that they arrive safely. If cattle are hauled by truck the driver must be skilful, for the animals may move one side and make it difficult to manage the truck. During transportation, cattle must not be exposed for too long to excessive heat or cold.
- Meat must be hauled in refrigerated vehicles to prevent spoilage. If the refrigeration unit fails, the meat must be moved quickly to another refrigerated area. Drivers must be alert for problems with refrigeration units.
- In transporting agricultural products diseased plants, animals and insect pests may be spread unknowingly. To prevent the spread of disease government regulation are applied to inspect vehicles crossing stateliness hauling agricultural products.

Types of Agricultural Carriers

Carriers are companies that transport goods from one place to another. There are different carriers that operate in the agricultural sector. These carriers provide different transportation means, which suited to the special nature of agricultural products. Some of these carriers include:

Truck carriers: Truck carriers range in size from light pick-up to heavy semi-trailer and with two trailers joined together behind a tractor. Trucks are equipped with special bodies for agricultural supplies and products that require special conditions.

Refrigerated trucks: To transport products such as milk, ice cream, meat, and frozen foods. Refrigerated trucks are used.

Bulk tank trucks: To haul various kinds of liquids — fruit juice, liquid feed, fertilizer, and motor fuel, perishable liquids like milk require refrigerated bulk tank trucks.

Bulk commodity trucks: These haul loose, dry materials such as feed, fertilizer, potatoes and fruit.

Flatbed trucks: These are used to haul a wide variety of agricultural material, from sacks of feed to lumber, from machinery to crates of chickens.

Livestock trucks: These are equipped with slatted sides for hauling cattle, goats, and sheep.

Container trucks: These have special bodies that can be lifted off and loaded on flat railroad cars for shipment. They are lifted back onto another container truck at the destination.

Rail carriers: Rail carriers are used for long distance shipping. There are many types of railroad cars to facilitate the shipping of agricultural supplies and products.

Open hopper cars: These are used for loose material such as chipped wood.

Boxcars: Used for bagged fertilizers, seed, ginned bales of cotton and many other products.

Covered hopper cars: Used for shipping grain.

Tank cars: These are used for shipping liquid fertilizer and fuel.

Refrigerated cars: Transport perishable food products such as fruit.

Water carriers: Transport agricultural supplies and products in ships and barges. Ships and barges often get bounced around by storms, so special packaging and loading techniques are important in preventing damage to products.

Air carriers: It is the most recent type of transportation for agricultural supplies and products. They are used mostly for highly perishable products and in emergency. Animal medicines, for example are shipped by air when out break of disease occur.

Other methods of shipping: Small packages can be sent by the regular mail service. Seed, small plants and nursery stock, animal medicines, spare parts, soil samples, grafting stock and other. Small packages can also be shipped on buses, which have regular, scheduled stops.

COMMUNICATION IN AGRIBUSINESS

Promotional activities in the agribusiness are designed to do one thing, sell more of the product or service. The marketing strategy incorporates various methods for informing customers and convincing them to buy. It is basically a communication process intended to modify customer behaviour toward a positive buying decision.

Advertising is mass communication with potential customers, usually through public communications media. Most advertising is product advertising designed to promote a specific product, service, or idea.

There is a wide variety of communications media ready to carry out the agribusiness's message.

Television is expensive and not widely used to communicate with farmers, except in predominantly rural areas for frequently purchased products with broad usage.

Radio is used more commonly by local agribusinesses, since it is less expensive and can target its farm audience by tying into agricultural programmes.

Other media forms include *handbills and flyers* sent directly to high-potential customers. Several organizations specialize in providing mailing lists of farmers in special categories.

Ads in *rural newspapers* are relatively inexpensive, but their actual value is very difficult to measure.

Coupons can give some agribusinesses a clue to the ad's effectiveness, but coupons do not lend themselves well to most general farm supplies.

Local, regional, and national *farm magazines* are an important method of communication with the farm customer.

Trade magazines geared to specific types of agribusinesses are also widely used to communicate with dealers and distributors.

The above media are widely used for communicating information regarding agribusiness. Communication is an important tool in agribusiness and it serves the best for creating linkage and improving the performance of the agribusiness firms.

STORAGE AND WAREHOUSING

STORAGE

Storage is very important facility considered in agribusiness, because most of the agricultural produces and products are perishable in nature.

Like transportation, storing is also a major function of marketing. Proper storing contributes a real asset to the products. It provides time utility to the product. If transportation is the process of transferring goods from one place to another, storage helps in keeping goods safely until they are needed. Both these function are complementary and entwined. Without Storing, transportation is not possible and storing is made possible by transportation Both these functions provide place and time utilities, which are an asset to any product waiting to be sold.

Meanings of Storing

Storing is holding a product in a healthy and safe place until it is needed either by manufacturer or consumer.

We can define storing as a function, which helps in preserving goods at one place until they are needed.

Agricultural products and supplies must be stored until needed. Since some farm and ranch products are seasonal, like apples and potatoes they must be stored until they are needed.

Agricultural products have distinct characteristics from non-agricultural products like they undergo respiration after harvest and other which makes storing the necessary function in agribusiness. In addition these agricultural products have different nature, which makes one different from the other which requires some considerations while storing different agricultural products.

The following are the main considerations that should be taken while storing.

- There is a great difference in the length of time products can be stored. Potatoes can be kept for months under proper conditions, while milk can be stored for only a short time. Many non-food farm commodities can be stored for very long periods without loss. For instance, items such as fertilizer and cotton if properly protected can be kept for many months or even year.
- The conditions under which some products are stored are very important. For example fresh fruits must be kept at cool temperature, but not cold enough to freeze them. Frozen foods must be kept at below freezing temperatures.

- In storage it is also important to protect commodities from insects, rodents and contamination.

Insects feed on the germ and endosperm of grains causing loss in weights as well as nutrients, contaminate by their dead bodies, cast skin, excreta and obnoxious odour, and also damage the containers and structures of the storage by causing tunneling in wooden parts resulting in the weakening of the structure. Insects also cause indirect damages by:

- Creating heat and migration of moisture
- Distribute parasites to man/certain tape worms use stored grain insects as intermediate hosts.
- It causes customer's resistance, which may lower the prestige.

Storage Functions in Agribusiness

Storage is generally required for agribusiness in the following situations:

- Production of most of the farm products is seasonal but their consumption is evenly spread throughout the year. So, storage is necessary to provide consistent supply with the demand that is to provide surplus storage to carry over supplies throughout the year.
- Storage is a necessary interim and repeated phase during transit of agricultural products from producer to processor and from processor to consumer. Farm products can be stored at the farm, at assembly point that is collection point from number of farms and at the processing and distribution areas.
- Agricultural products need to be stored from one harvest to next to be used as seed thus, demanding additional carry over as safeguard against a following crop of low yield or poor quality.
- Storage facilities are needed for overcoming unfavorable price situations or for speculative purposes. Farmers can benefit if they can keep part of their crop to await

seasonally higher prices. Most traders who take possession of produce need some storage space so that they can choose the best time to resell.

- Storing is necessary to safeguard against shortage and famines, to provide surplus storage to carry over supplies in the year of low production.
- Processing plants must have stocks of their raw materials conveniently at hand to ensure smooth and continuous production that keeps continued customer service and keeps machinery and staff from standing idle because of delays in the arrival of supplies.

Storage Structures

The storage structures may be of traditional storage structure, improved structure, and modern storage structure. We will see one by one in the following paragraphs.

Traditional Storage Structures

In our country mainly two types of traditional storage structures are known where farmers use to store their seeds and grains.

- The one that is used by farmers in the central, northern, southern and western parts of Ethiopia is the above ground bin locally known as *gotera*. It is made up of bamboo sticks, wood and mud. The structure is made on raised platform supported on wooden pillars.
- The other type of storage used in the eastern part of our country, is Hararghe, the flask-shaped traditional underground pit with variable dimensions. The storage pits are usually dug in sandy or stony soils with gentle topography and where there is less water drainage problem and less hazard of soil collapsing into the pits. The contacts of the grain with wet inner pit walls often leads to moisture ingress into the intergranular space elevating both the grain moisture content and the relative humidity inside the pit. Besides, respiration by insect

pests, micro-fungi, micro-organism and the living grain itself produces high temperature and water activity. Such a pit leads to molding and grain deterioration. The grain stored in the underground storage pit is often mixed with collapsing soil from the walls and this affects its purity, market and nutritional value. It is also inconvenient to remove grain for consumption or sale at frequent intervals.

Improved Storage Structures

These structures are simply the traditional storage structure with some modifications to keep grains from quantitative and qualitative deterioration.

- The above ground bin can be modified by lining with plastic raising the platform at least at a height of 80 cm and placing rat proofing cones on all the four pillars to avoid rats entering the storage structure.

This is not the only method of improving the above ground bins, other materials such as bricks, concrete blocks etc. roofing and insulating materials can be used taking into account the purchasing capacity of the peasants.

- Underground storage pits may be improved by extending the neck of the pit above ground level with clay or even a concrete slab to minimize the risk of rainwater penetrating at this point. This risk can be further reduced by digging trenches around and away from the pit to remove rainwater from the area as quickly as possible. The floor of the pit may be strengthened with stones or concrete the walls may be solidified with cow dung. Plastic sheeting could be applied to the walls and the floor, but this is not easy and it is probably more practical to put the grain into plastic sacks and stock these in the pit.

Modern Storage Structures

The modern facility for storing grains in bulk is *silo*. Silos are constructed from steel or reinforced concrete. There are a cluster of adjoining silos in any modern large capacity processing plant. These silos may or may not be of different configurations. These silos are generally circular with conical or flat bottom.

WAREHOUSING

The function of storage is performed through housing or storing the products properly. The place where the goods are stored is known as a warehouse.

Definition: Warehouse is a building or room for storing goods. Thus storage is a function of marketing and warehouse is the tool with this function is performed.

Some authors take warehouses as one type of storage. The first category of storage, which is used for keeping the bulk produce of non-perishable commodities like, food grains, oilseeds, cotton and similar products as a warehouse. The second type of storage meant primarily for perishable and semi-perishable commodities call it cold storage.

Functions of Warehouses

Warehousing embraces a number of functions such as assembling, dividing and storing products, and preparing them for reshipping.

Types of Warehousing

The different kinds of warehouses can be divided in different ways. We will see their division on the basis of ownership and special provision.

I. *Warehouses*

(a) Private warehouse is a firm or manufacturer or trader who operates a warehouse exclusively for his own purpose.

- It is more likely to be an advantages if;
- a company moves a large volume of product through a warehouse;
- there is very little if any seasonal fluctuation in this flow; and

- the goods have special handling or storage requirement.

(b) Public warehouse rents space to individuals or firms needing storage. The costs are variable customer pays only when they use it. The charge depends on area occupied, period used, special nature of the commodity etc.

(c) Co-operative warehouses – The ownership of these houses is vested in the hands of a primary cooperative society. This type of warehousing method is believed to provide a high advantage to farmers in villages.

II. *Specialty warehouses*

Certain products have to be stored under special conditions. To meet this need specialized warehouses came into operation.

(a) General merchandise warehouses.

(b) Special commodity warehouses constructed to house certain commodities, which require special treatment. For example grains, cotton, wool, etc. require special condition like maintenance of temp., humidity etc.

(c) Refrigerated warehouses (cold storage): This is a latest technology used to store perishable products.

Importance of Warehousing for Agricultural Products

The importance of warehousing is felt for the agricultural products since they are mostly perishable in nature. Warehouses are maintained in order to keep the agricultural products safely. Moreover, the quality of agricultural products can be maintained through well-furnished warehouses.

Summary

- The term infrastructure has different meanings in different disciplines. Simply it can be defined as a large-scale technological system, consisting of immovable physical facilities and delivering an essential public or private service(s) through the storage, conversion and/ or transportation of certain commodities. The infrastructure includes those parts and subsystems necessary for fulfilling the primary storage, transportation, and/or conversion function as well as those supporting proper executions of these functions.

- Infrastructure is a key factor for performance and for improving the efficiency of any system. Marketing infrastructure involves physical and institutional infrastructure. Physical market infrastructure can be put under two categories:
  - (a) directly related to marketing; and
  - (b) indirectly related to marketing.
- Infrastructures are largely responsible for increase in marketing efficiency. The important items of infrastructure for the growth of marketing of agricultural produce include — processing, transportation, wholesale assembly, godown/storage/cold storage facility and warehousing, roads, regulated agricultural markets besides rural market, marketing finance, other agencies for disposal and procurement (like regulated markets/ cooperative marketing/ commodity corporations/state agencies, etc).
- Transportation is shipping materials to required places or getting materials to where they are required. There are five major modes of transportation: airlines, motor carriers, pipelines, railroads and water carriers. Each of these modes has distinct characteristics that give them advantage over the others. Which method is best depends on the freight hauled, cost, speed, reliability, capability, capacity, length of haul, and flexibility.
- Most of agricultural products and supplies are transported by truck, rail or water. Air transportation is not commonly used except for certain specialized products

and supplies which are highly perishable products such as flowers and fish are shipped frequently by air. Since many farm products especially food are delicate as well as perishable they must be moved carefully as well as quickly. Delays in getting highly perishables to the processors result in spoilage, making the products worthless.

- Promotional activities in the agribusiness are designed to do one thing, sell more of the product or service. The marketing strategy incorporates various methods for informing customers and convincing them to buy. It is basically a communication process intended to modify customer behaviour toward a positive buying decision. There is a wide variety of communications media ready to carry out the agribusiness's message. Communication is an important tool in agribusiness and it serves the best for creating linkage and improving the performance of the agribusiness firms.
- Storing is holding a product in a healthy and safe place until it is needed either by manufacturer or consumer. Agricultural products have different nature which makes one different from the other which requires some considerations while storing different agricultural products.
- The place where the goods are stored is known as a warehouse. Warehouses have a function of assembling, dividing and storing products, and preparing them for reshipping.

Self-Learning Activity

Try to answer the following questions on your own:

1. Explain the need for infrastructure in agribusiness.
2. What are the advantages of transport?
3. Describe the role of communication in agribusiness.
4. What is the importance of warehousing in agribusiness?

4

Socio-Cultural Factors in Agribusiness

Although the physical nature of an environment primarily determines peoples' mode of life and the general nature of their agriculture, racial or tribal differences have an important secondary influence.

Agriculture and agribusiness is generally affected by the differing characteristics of various peoples, and in particular by their stage of advancement in technology and their social structure, beliefs, traditions and customs.

Level of Technology

In Ethiopia farming is characterized by dependence on traditional tools and farming practices which affects productivity of the agricultural sector. For instance, land is prepared by oxen drawn plough that will not provide the land to be porous for the movement of air, water and root that affects the growth of plants, planting is done by manual broadcasting which hampers effective weeding and spraying activities. Weeding is done manually, and harvesting also performed manually with the help of sickle. Threshing is performed by animals trampling the harvested crop. In addition, agricultural produce is transported by animals and human power, low application of modern input, poor animal breeds etc.

Land Fragmentation

The increasing population of rural Ethiopia and the limited total land area, especially in the highlands farming area has been the cause for declining landholding of farmers which in turn results the households to produce seldom enough crop to meet their family's consumption requirement. As to landhold is too small to produce any marketable surplus under the prevailing conditions, subsistence and survival are the over tiding concern of the farmers. This resulted in lack of cash for investment purchase of commercial inputs and purchase of oxen for land preparation.

In addition, fragmentation of scattered pieces of land contributes to the difficulties of getting effective soil conservation measures implemented and increases the labor and time required in agricultural advisory work. The small size and irregular shape of the plots often results in waste of land and hampers cultivation by any other means than hand tools.

Increased Population and Density

Population density and increase may markedly affect farming systems, or their effects on the natural resources. In Africa the formerly relative sparse population practicing shifting cultivation solely for subsistence, was in balance with its environment. Latterly the increase in population coupled with greatly increased production of cash crop and livestock has caused severe pressure on the land in certain areas. As a result restorative fallow become impracticable, or so much reduced as to be ineffective and the soil rapidly deteriorates, yields decline with the result that land is no longer capable of adequately supporting the people. Similarly, in many pastoral areas increasing human and stock population have accelerated the ill-effects of poor farming.

Unfortunately in most parts of African population increase has not been accompanied by the evolution of improved farming system, and the common picture is one of the deterioration of the land and other natural resources. From agricultural point of view the remedies lies in the evolution of better farming systems and husbandry techniques.

Social Structure, Traditions and Beliefs

Among most African peoples agriculture was until recently practiced primarily for subsistence and farming system formed an inherent, essential part of the culture of the people being intimately bound up with other elements of that culture. This influence of the general cultural pattern on agriculture has too a considerable extent persisted in modern times. Despite the wide spread production of crops for sale, farming in many countries is still in the nature of a traditional occupation than a business. Farming systems may be directly influenced by this inter-relationship between agriculture and other cultural elements and beliefs.

Living in a group, clan or tribe that peoples living strictly in accordance with the custom of that group the individual was expected to act according to tribal custom; there was little scope for initiative or deviation from an accepted pattern, because individual initiative was frowned upon and commonly incurred reprisals. As a result there were virtually no agricultural innovators or experimentalists and practically no exceptionally good farmers from whom others might learn.

In recent times tribal customs and authority have been declining, group life has been disintegrating and people are living more and as individuals. Nevertheless the customs and habits of centuries cannot be changed in a few years.

Land Tenure

Uncertainty about the possible communalization of land and the continuing land redistribution erodes the incentive to invest in permanent conservation and improvement on individual holdings.

RESOURCE UTILIZATION IN AGRIBUSINESS

Resource Classification

The word resource means any good or services that can be used to produce a good capable of satisfying a human want. A natural resource is simply a resource provided by nature, a good existing in the universe, yet not limited solely to physical things since such phenomena as tides, winds and energy of the sun in nature have value until they have been discovered and an economic use has been found for them.

Natural resources are then a function not only of their physical existence, but also depends upon our knowledge of them and the technology of use plus our ability to make economic use of them as sources of want satisfying goods and services.

- Of the wide array of resources around us some are land, water, minerals, plant and animals.

Natural Resource Classification

Natural resources are classified as follows:

Fund (stock) resources

These are resources, which are fixed in quantity, and using them depletes the amounts remaining. Many of our natural resources are of this type: coal, oil, natural gas, sand and stone, iron ore and other minerals, and similar non-renewable resources whose use forever reduces their remaining quantities.

Flow resources

These are resources where their present uses do not prevent possible future use because the available quantity is constantly being replenished. In using the winds power, heat energy from the sun or a flow water stream does not disturb their continued flow, the amounts available for other uses is left undiminished. This group includes resources such as sunlight, wind, rain, tides and flowing water.

Note: A simple fund or flow classification does not adequately serve to describe all natural resources, however many other important resources exhibit some characteristics of both these groupings.

- Growing maturing plants (the flow) may be harvested without damaging the productivity of the parent stock (the fund). The product flow can be maintained indefinitely increased or decreased, depending on the harvesting rate and the manner in which both the fund and flow are managed.
- Our forests, ranges, livestock, fish and wildlife yield an annual product which may be taken without harm to the productive sources of that output. Yet each can be used in ways that may either enhance or diminish the quantity (& productivity) of that fund resource, with production increase or decrease following in uses or use rate.
- Soil itself although most frequently viewed as fund resource also has some of the characteristics of flow resources. Management practices may have the deliberate objective of reducing, maintaining or improving the levels of plant nutrients held in the soil, depending upon whether current practices use those nutrients at a greater, equal or lesser rate than their inflow to the soil.

This is to be noted that forest cutting can be so intensive in one period of time that future yields are reduced, even eliminated entirely. Rangel and can be overgrazed to the extent that grass re-growth and production declines in later years

Resource Utilization

The physical facts of a resource existence and their capabilities to satisfy human wants do not establish the criteria by which those natural resources are used. In the utilization of any natural (other) resource we can not escape making choices as to whether or not to use a resource, the rate at which to use it and the purpose of its use, causing them to be economic questions requiring economic criteria for their solution.

Resource Inventories

Of all the natural resources that exist, what we do now about them? How much of cash is there? How much do we use? How much can we use? Are there better uses for them? Will there be adequate supply in the future? And of what importance are the numerous "if" conditions that must be dealt with in projections into the future?

Attempts at identifying the amounts of specific natural resource that we now have and may or may not have in the future, are not, confusing; interpretational liberties taken with technically develop terms frequently make them so.

Take, for instance, the abstraction in the Figure 4.1, a conceptual framework that can be applied to any natural (or other) resource.

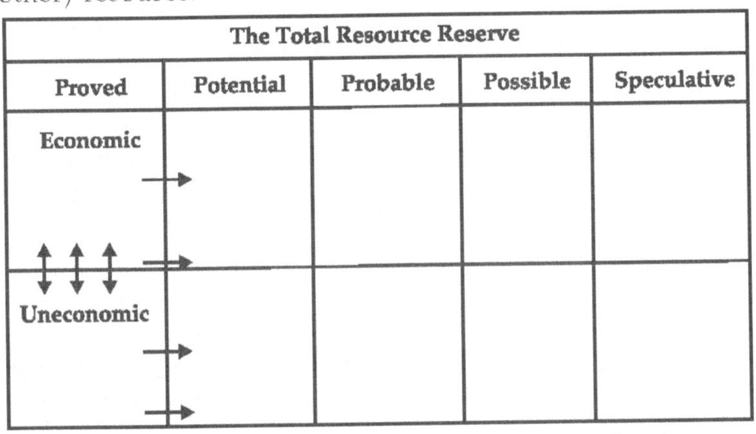

Fig 4.1: **A natural resource inventory classification**

- The area of the box demonstrated the total physical quantity of a specific resource as it exists in the natural state.
- Proved reserve depends upon past production and exploratory work that the size of the deposit known with considerable certainty.
- Potential reserves are less certain, depending on the type of resource estimates are developed from out-cropping,

test drillings or other sampling, production data and projections from geological evidence.

- Probable reserves: unexplored area may closely adjoin a producing area; inferences may be drawn as to the quantity that might be found.
- Possible reserves: with their estimated quantities being based upon underground structural similarities with a producing area nearby.
- Speculative resource: are the most uncertain of all. There is lack of geological testing in an area forces speculation.

The mere fact of physical presence, however, is insufficient. We must be able to take the resource from its present location, with whatever refining and processing is required and get it marketed. If this can be done without sacrificing other, more valuable goods and services, it is economically feasible. If not, its high cost would cause the resource to be unutilized.

Note: Economic feasibility is determined by extraction and related technology, price and cost.

A primitive technology, based primarily on had labor, for instant may prevent any use of a resource. As capital investment in improved technology makes possible the movement of sufficient quantities of the resource-bearing material, costs per unit of extracted product fall low enough that it becomes feasible to utilize the resource, as indicated by the line running horizontally through the diagram. The more technology is improved the farther downward the line will be pushed, reflecting the fact that it has become possible to reach to deeper levels or lower concentrations for the resource, as indicated by the downward pointing arrows.

The other important element in determining economic feasibility is price. As the price of the extracted product increases the horizontal line is shifted downward, as it decreases the horizontal line shifts upward; indicated by the upward and downward pointing arrows. The higher the price the deeper we can go in extracting the resource on the other had a falling price will make uneconomic the harvesting of this resources at the depths and concentrations that formerly were feasible.

With population increases and possible new uses for the resource, the demand curve for the resource will shift to the right, causing its price to rise, *ceteris paribus*. Not only does this cause additional quantities of the proved reserve to become economic, the higher price will encourage more intensive searching for new sources and further effort at improving the technology of detection, as well as its extraction, causing to shift of the vertical boundary to the right. Proved reserves are thus expanded in spite of the fact that past and current use has constantly been withdrawing from the physical quantity originally available.

Resource supplies

Having some knowledge of the physical amount of various resources that are present is of value only as a limit. The physical supply of any resource may be defined as the total quantity provided by nature. But that would include the total area of the diagram above, which for most natural resources, has little relationship to the amounts used. The concept of greatest relevance is that of economic supply part of the physical supply that is used for want of satisfaction. We could attempt to equate this physical quantity with the economically feasible portion of the proved reserve, but this is a total concept – the sum of both the amount actually used and the amount unused. If we limit ourselves to meaning that amount of the resource actually use within some time-period (annually for instance), we have been pushed to considering the equilibrium quantity, a single point on the supply curve of that resource.

With this view of economic supply, we can more readily recognize the importance of both supply and demand upon how intensively we use our natural resources, and at what rates they are being consumed in the production process. The demand and supply concept are fundamental to understand changes that occur in our reserves. They make clear that expansions and contractions of the economic supplies of natural resources are caused by resource price changes, which are the result of changes in either or both supply & demand functions.

Resources values

Natural resources in themselves have no value; they are valued, and command a price only because they are capable of producing goods and services people want and are willing to pay for. Thus, the demand for a resource is derived demand. It is derived from the fact that the resource can produce something else, the demand for which gets reflected back to the resource itself. Hence the demand for land depends on the intensity of our demand for the products of land food and fiber, aesthetic, or other valued quality.

To arrive at a dollar value of a resource, we must determine the costs and returns arising with the use of that resource, and the net returns resulting from its use.

Resource productivity surely must affect the price one is willing to pay. Resource valuation is made by adjusting or discounting the net returns back to their present values.

Resource conservation

To some, the conservation of natural resources is accomplished by a willful reduction in the rate at which these resources are used, leading to the concept of saving. And to this is frequently added the admonition that we must "save for future generation". Faithful adherence to this dictum, result in perpetual non-use because we are unable to specify which generation in the near or far-off future may have the privilege of use.

To save resources so as to have a large quantity available in the future, is of questionable value, because new discoveries or new technology yet unavailable, may result in very large increase of usable reserves or new alternative sources of the same service thus, an economic waste of presently valuable resource.

The conservation of natural resources is an important part of the economic problem of dealing with scarcity by making the proper choices, accomplished only by weighing economic alternatives. As consumers economize in their production choices, the basic requirements of efficiency in resource conservation have been met.

Efficiency in resource use dictates that we use our resources at the time and at the rate, and in those uses where their contribution to consumer satisfaction is the greatest. There by preventing wasteful use.

We have optimized natural resources conservation when we have so distributed the rates at which those resources are used that we have maximized the present value of the future stream of their net social benefits.

The economic meaning of conservation takes the future into account by answering the question: what is the best rate at which to utilize any resource so as to maximize net social benefit over time? This can be answered by comparing values between different periods.

OPPORTUNITIES IN AGRIBUSINESS

Business of Job Hunting

Finding an appropriate job requires a great deal of common sense and perseverance. There are a great many factors contributing to an individual's success in agribusiness and the true professional will meet the challenges presented by all of them. Therefore, after completion of your degree you are expected to be a marketable product. Therefore the emphasis of this chapter is to introduce you how to search for a job, what we generally call the business of job hunting. In order to understand the aspects of this chapter please go through the section patiently.

In a real sense, looking for a job constitutes a business proposition in and of itself. A great deal of time and money have been invested in what you must believe is a marketable product-yourself. Now that product has been completed (though, of course, you will continue to develop through a lifetime), the task before you is to sell the product as effectively as possible. It may interest you to know that the field you are about to enter has much to offer and that your training has prepared you to meet its challenges.

Challenge of Expanding Opportunities

Agriculture is the only major renewable resource and major economic activity in Ethiopia. Properly managed, it offers the potential for a constant export that regenerates itself and can even grow annually; whereas, most other natural resources are gradually depleted. World demand for our agricultural production continues to grow, as world population increases and an increasing world standard of living put foreign customers in a better position to buy our agricultural products. Because of the natural advantages of Ethiopia in food crop production, coffee production; and because of the economic development policy of Ethiopia (agricultural development–led industrialization) encourages productivity and efficiency through cooperatives, there is every reason to believe that Ethiopian agriculture will continue to improve, offering outstanding opportunities for aggressive well-trained young agriculturists and cooperators.

Finding a Place in the Scheme

As the opportunities increase, it becomes more and more important for you to develop a strong sense of yourself, of your place in the scheme. A positive self-image begins with a strong sense of the qualities and background you have to offer.

What you have to offer

For one thing, you can contribute a great deal of energy and enthusiasm. You have at least some technical agricultural competency that your employer can build on. Of course, there are endless things to learn, but your employer is expecting to help you learn the things you need to know, and your college training has been geared to teach you to learn quickly and fully. Your interest in and experience with cooperative and agriculture is also valuable to your employer. At school you may have made many contacts on whom you can call if your company needs specialized advice. In short, your employer is interested in buying your loyalty, competence, enthusiasm, and willingness to learn and work.

Selecting a company

The decision whether to work in a large corporate organization or a smaller local agribusiness is often a difficult one. Predictably, both prospects offer advantages and disadvantages; the final choice rests on the values and interests of the individual involved.

Larger firms tend to offer more prestige, particularly among students as they compare job offers. Even later, mention of employment with a well-known firm tends to generate a spark of recognition in conversation.

In addition, larger firms are usually more formally organized. Each job has a title and a job description. There is a formal; often extensive fringe benefit plan, and a training program may be detailed in advance. Larger firms often require their employees to move from one location to another for promotions. Even at one location, there is usually ample opportunity for travel, sometimes extensively.

Smaller firms, on the other hand, offer much more of a "down home" flavor, since everyone in the company may know everyone else. There may be almost a family atmosphere, with all employees on a first-name basis. Since the local company usually has few locations, moving is not necessary. Power structures and benefit plans may not be so formal, travel is less frequent, and advancement paths less clear. Responsibilities are often broader and delegated earlier.

Training programs are usually on the job, but working closely with an experienced pro and having broader responsibilities earlier can be a very effective way to learn. Even very small, family-owned firms can offer good opportunities. Of course, advancement in the family-owned agribusiness may be limited unless provision is made for partial ownership after a few years.

Selecting a job

Finding and deciding on your first job will be a very important and exciting step in your professional agribusiness career. In all likelihood, you have been preparing yourself for several months to several years for taking that first job, yet you may be somewhat confused about the kind of job you want or what firm you would like to work for.

Some new entries into the job market half expect agribusinesses to inundate them with job offers. When this does not occur, they should not interpret it as an indication that opportunities are lacking. It simply means that they must look for the opportunities rather than waiting for the opportunities to search them out.

Some people find it easier to get job offers than others because they have more contacts, more experience, a stronger record, or a more pleasant personality than others. Those who are not in this position must simply work harder to catch up.

Notice that we have not talked about finding the right job. There is no one right job. Most people could enjoy and prosper with many different alternatives. The difference between best and second best may be slight, so the important thing is to select an acceptable and appropriate opportunity. One of the most valuable experiences is to go to agribusiness manages in your home community and ask them what you can except from different types of agribusiness jobs. You will gain useful general information and good job leads form such people.

Setting objectives

The first step in the job-selection process is to set both personal and professional objectives for yourself. Think through what you want out of life. What kinds of things do you enjoy? Do you want to travel, and how much? Do you want to work outdoors or in an office? How important are money, power, prestige? Do you have a strong geographical preference? If you are married, your spouse will play an extremely important role in answering these questions. It is a good idea to put your thoughts on paper. This may help to clarify some issues, such as values and priorities, that are partially hidden even from yourself.

Developing a Strategy

Once you have decided what your goals and objectives are, you must develop a strategy for finding job opportunities that will satisfy your objectives. This means developing an action plan that specifies how to proceed. Will you mass-produce resumes, or will you depend largely on personal contacts? Will you devote most of your attention to campus interviews, or will you go to the field yourself? You may want to talk with your counselor or placement service as you develop your strategy.

Budget time and Money

Be sure to budget adequate resources to do justice to your marketing effort. After all, you have invested much time (several years?) and money (thousands of dollars?) in this product. It does not make sense to wait until graduation or to consider only a few options in marketing yourself. Plan to spend money (borrowed if necessary), to make long-distance calls, and to visit employers. Start early enough to do it properly; several months before you are ready to go to work.

Where to look for jobs

Your choice of where to look for job opportunities will be influenced not only by your objectives but by the type of agribusiness that seems best. Many students make the error of looking only at agribusinesses that send professional recruiters to the school. While many of these firms offer excellent job opportunities, usually only larger firms can afford to recruit formally and many of their opportunities are limited to sales jobs.

School placement service

Many schools do an excellent job of matching firms and students by organizing and facilitating job interviews. This is an excellent opportunity and should be used early and extensively by the student. Students should check this service for interesting possibilities at least weekly during their last year.

Professors and teachers

Instructors are often the best single source of information. Often they have a great number of personal contracts. Since they know both you and potential employers, they can be very helpful in locating possible jobs. Even if they do not have a list of firms that are currently hiring, they know the firms that have employed past graduates, and so are in a position to divulge some good leads. Do not hesitate to ask for help. Remember, the success of school's cooperative programme depends on successful placement of its graduates. Your advisors want you to get a good job.

Trade associations

Nearly every agribusiness industry is represented in national (and often state) trade organizations. The offices of these organizations are in touch with members' needs. Some organizations go so far as to publish lists of available job openings. Libraries have special books listing national associations and their addresses.

Government agencies

In Ethiopia, the government itself employs many agriculturists and cooperators. The Ministry of Rural and

Agriculture, Federal and Regional Cooperative Agency, and Public Agro Processing Industries are typical examples. Usually, it is best to contact a representative of the agency in which you are interested to get additional information. Sometimes students must take civil service exams to qualify for these jobs.

Employment agencies

The number of private firms that specialize in finding employees for agribusinesses are increasing. While most of these firms are quite reputable, some are less so. Reputable agencies usually work only with employers who are willing to pay the fees for the agency's services.

Other students and friends

Some of the best information may come from others who are also in the job market. Some students worry about competing with each other, but this is seldom a problem. Each person is so different from every other person that the same jobs generally do not appeal to everyone. Work together and compare notes. Often relatives and friends back home have some contacts.

Personal contacts

Your own personal contact network is likely to be your most productive source of information. Aggressive pursuit of many sources often uncovers unusual possibilities. One lead sometimes flows directly into another.

Resumes (Curriculum Vitae-CV)

A resume is a written summary of your personal, educational, and professional qualifications. Its purpose is to present prospective employers with enough information to determine whether they are interested in you. In some ways, it is a formal advertisement for yourself.

Resumes are developed individually, so no two are alike. However, most include identification of the candidate, career objectives, personal and professional experience that might be valuable to the job, employment history, and sometimes references with whom the employer can check. Usually, resumes are limited to a single page. A recent photo may or may not be printed on the resume or attached to it. It is important to include a personalized cover letter for each company that will receive the resume. References should be drawn from non-family members who know you well. Among the references, be sure to include a previous employer who knows you well enough to evaluate you, but get the employer's permission first.

A sample resume given below for your understanding and for further action while you are finding job opportunities in agribusiness.

Sample Resume

DAVID K. DANIEL

CURRENT ADDRESS	PERMANENT ADDRESS
Haile G/ Silassie Street	P. O. Box 2000
Arada Subcity	AMBO UNIVERSITY, WEST SHOA
Phone: 0911111111	Phone: 011-236-31-62

PERSONAL DATA

Birth Date: July 20, 1979

Sex: Female

Height: 1.62 meter

Weight: 56 kg

Health: Excellent

Marital Status: Single

Nationality: Ethiopian

JOB OBJECTIVITY

I am interested in a rewarding and challenging business career in cooperative promotion, in cooperative auditing, in sales or marketing etc. I would eventually be interested in a managerial position.

EDUCATIONAL BACKGROUND

Senior in Cooperative Management/ Accounting and Auditing

Major Grade Points: 3.82

Cumulative GPA: 3.75

Graduation Date: July, 2009

Have taken wide background of courses including:

Agronomy, Animal Husbandry, Advanced English, Management, Business Statistics, Business Mathematics, Business Communication, Computer and its application and Information system courses.

ACTIVITIES AND HONORS

President of student council, AMBO UNIVERSITY, for one year

Chainman of Student Saving and Credit Cooperative Society

Honorary certificate of environmental protection and sustainable development

WORK EXPERIENCE

Five years of work experience as a production manager, Tsinat Factory, AMBO

Four years of work experience as Elementary School Teacher, Ambo Woreda.

REFERENCES AND ADDITIONAL INFORMATION FURNISHED UPON REQUEST

Some tips for a successful career

There is no one clear path to a successful career in agribusiness. It seems trite to say that dedication, hard work, perseverance, and loyalty are necessary, yet the authors cannot resist the temptation to share a few tips that have proved useful to the many graduates they have worked with over the years.

Begin at the grass-roots level

Most people begin their professional careers in agribusiness physically handling products and servicing customers. This grass-roots experience is invaluable for understanding the fundamentals of agribusiness management. A strong argument can be made that these experiences are a prerequisite for any significant advancement into management. This phase of the professional career helps a person understand firsthand what it means to carry out management directions, to communicate with customers effectively, and to deal with the hectic activity of peak-season responsibility.

Pay your dues

Accept the initiation period during which all new employees must prove themselves to become accepted by their peers. This period is particularly troublesome for young college people who have difficulty relating to older worker who have no college training. It sometimes means being the butt of practical jokes and accepting less desirable jobs, but this period should not last forever, so grin and bear it.

Learn the power structure

In every agribusiness there are individuals who wield far more power than their formal position would suggest. Their power may result from seniority, proximity to real power, personality, or a number of other things. Although it may not be wise to play politics, it is equally unwise to ignore powerful people in organizations.

Make your boss look good

Nothing can get you more attention and favorable evaluations (including pay raises) than making your boss look good. If you can get your boss promoted, there will be an opening for you. Or, alternatively, the boss may take you along with him or her. When talking to others in the organization, speak of your boss with respect. Compliment your boss when appropriate, and express gratitude when you genuinely appreciate something.

Be a team member

A successful agribusiness operates as a team. Each member has specific assigned tasks, but the job is not complete when an individual finishes an individual task. The total team must work toward completion of the total task. This often means helping others, even at the temporary expense of postponing completion of your task.

Be visible

While teamwork is critical, it is also important to do something that is clearly your own. That is, make sure that at least some of the results of your efforts are noticeable to others. Sometimes this will involve some small extra project, which you might have initiated on your own; that you believe might be valuable to the company.

Make suggestions

As a professional, you have a responsibility to watch for weak areas and suggest improvements. Do not be afraid to voice your ideas; suggestions make it clear that you care. Make your suggestions tactfully, and do not expect your idea to suddenly change the way the business is run. Have the patience to wait for an idea to take hold, and do not take lack of response as a personal rebuff. Remember to separate criticism of your ideas from criticism of you as a person. Plant the seed and let it grow.

Recognize that change is threatening

People become accustomed to and comfortable with certain methods of operating a business. Whenever someone suggests changes, people may become threatened and resist change. Recognize this principle and promote change cautiously.

Weight the cost a being right

Whenever conflict or differences of opinion arise, you must decide whether to push your ideas, and if so, how far. Even when you are absolutely certain you are correct, you may decide that your gain from pushing your idea is more than outweighed by the resulting ill feeling from the other person or persons. Weigh this carefully.

Allow people to save face

In situations where a conflict arises and it becomes obvious you are in the right, avoid the temptation of forcing the other person to admit that he or she is wrong. Although there might be a lot of personal satisfaction in such and action, embarrassment of the other person can create bitter feelings that you will have to live with for a long time. Always leave the other person with a way of saving face.

Manage expectations

All discontent is relative to expectation. If you tell someone that you can make a delivery by 3 p.m. and you arrive at 3:15, the customer is likely to be frustrated. If you promise delivery by 3:30 and arrive at 3:15, the customer will be impressed by your promptness. This is not to suggest that you should regularly underestimate your ability. It means that you should be realistic and not overstate what you can do.

Ask for help

It is amazing what people will do when you simply ask them, yet pride or ignorance often keeps people from asking for help directly. This technique is especially helpful for people who are new on the job. Experienced personnel are often eager to play a parental role and may even be protective.

Always give a little extra

For fast movement and a rewarding professional career, it pays to do a bit more than is expected of you in every aspect of your job. Do not leave at the stroke of 5 p.m; stay a bit later. Get there a few minutes early each day. Make an extra phone call. Always doing a little bit more than what is expected can generate real benefits.

Professional Agribusiness Management

A profession is an occupation requiring specialized knowledge, which in turn requires long and intensive training.

Professional agribusiness managers require the formal study of management methods as they apply to the agribusiness. Professionals must learn how to analyze, decide, plan, execute, and lead. Some of this learning is formal, in the classroom, or in seminars and workshops. Some of this learning, perhaps the greater part of it, is experiential, or on the job; while some of the learning is personal, through reading books and self-examination. A professional manager is continually striving to become better and more effective.

In addition a profession requires a certain code of conduct from its members. Although agribusiness managers do not have to take formal vows, there is clearly a code of conduct expected of professional managers. Legal regulations form one kind of base for acceptable management conduct but ethical expectations go much deeper than simple legalities. Managers have a great moral and ethical responsibility to employees, stockholders, and the general public for effectively and efficiently managing the resources under their command. Professional agribusiness managers accept this responsibility.

A profession is also an occupation engaged in for financial rewards. Agribusiness managers have great opportunities for significant financial rewards. Owners and investors are fully aware of the importance of good management in protecting and increasing the value of their investment. Compensation in the form of salary and bonuses can make agribusiness management a very rewarding profession. Agribusiness management is a profession. Becoming a professional manager of an agribusiness is an exciting challenge to meet.

Summary

- Agribusiness offers growing almost unlimited opportunities for aggressive well trained young agriculturists. Job-hunting means it is searching for a job. You don't have to expect jobs to search for you, rather it is you who is to search for a job. Yet job opportunities are not likely to seek out the applicant. A productive job search requires a systematic and logical approach much as a marketing manager would plan to market product. Objectives should be carefully thought through, a strategy mapped out, and the plan executed. An integral part of the job search involves seeking employment information from a variety of sources and then sending resumes and seeking personal interviews.

- Finding an appropriate job requires a great deal of common sense and perseverance. There are a great many factors contributing to an individual's success in agribusiness or in other future career, and the true professional will meat the challenges presented by all of them.
- Resumes or Curriculum Vitae-CV is a written summary of your personal, educational, and professional qualifications. Its purpose is to present prospective employers with enough information to determine whether they are interested in you. In some ways, it is a formal advertisement for yourself.
- A profession is an occupation requiring specialized knowledge, which in turn requires long and intensive training. Professional agribusiness managers require the formal study of management methods as they apply to the agribusiness. Professionals must learn how to analyze, decide, plan, execute, and lead. Some of this learning is formal, in the classroom, or in seminars and workshops. Some of this learning, perhaps the greater part of it, is experiential, or on the job; while some of the learning is personal, through reading books and self-examination.

Self-Learning Activity

Try to answer the following questions on your own:

1. What are the social factors that affect agribusiness.
2. Give an account of resource values?
3. What is the scope for professional agribusiness management?

5

Agricultural Extension Services

Meaning and Definition

Agricultural extension is the oldest extension service established in 1944, during industrial revolution. Agricultural extension is a difficult term to define precisely because it is applied in different ways to accomplish a wide variety of objectives. The term therefore has a variety of meaning to different people.

In most countries extension is deployed, as an instrument to achieve policy goals, for which agricultural extension is a typical example. Agricultural policy in most countries is directed towards development of agricultural industries, not for helping individual farmers. Usually export goals, national food securities, cheap food supplies for urban dwellers, are given priorities above the welfare of farmers. Extension activities typically focus on "advisory work" as in the UK and Germany; while the America tradition the term "extension education" is used to emphasize that they are engaging in educational activity which seeks to teach people to solve problems by "extending" information to them.

It is appropriate to first look into the various meanings attached to the word "Extension".

The word "Extension" is a very common word. If you refer to any standard and ordinary dictionary the literal meaning is associated with meaning like: to extend; to enlarge; to expand; to further, to advice or, to counsel etc.

Extension stands for "the action or process of enlarging or extending something". It could be extension of area, time or space. These ordinary meanings of the word "extension" then can be made to expand to some sort of educational activities.

The use of the word "extension" derives from an educational development in the second half of the nineteenth century. The overt (plain) use of the notion of "extending" relevant and useful information to the adult population at large, however, predates the university extension movement.

From different authors of Agricultural extension we can have different definitions. However, let's take it as agricultural extension involves the provision of or transfer of something (i.e. ideas, advice, information, knowledge, skills); and that the activity of begins with that of provision.

Van den Ban and Hawkins, (1988; p. 312) define extension as "A conscious communication of information to help people from sound opinions and make good decisions".

Swanson et al. (1984; p. 1) define Agricultural Extension as "A service or system, which assists farm people, through educational procedures in improving farming methods and techniques, increasing production efficiency and income, bettering their level of living, and lifting the social and educational standard of rural life".

Common Elements in the Definitions

These definitions of agricultural extension suggest that it involve the provision of "something", usually said to be "useful, necessary, new, or appropriate".

Therefore, among the common elements enshrined in the definitions are:

1. Extension is an intervention, which emphasizes that it is a planned, systematically designed goal-oriented activity. Extension uses and depends very much on communication for all its activities.
2. *Communication as an instrument or tool to bring change:* The only instrument in extension to promote change is communication. Hence, extension is a communication intervention, which aims at changing people's behaviour and attitude, but not the farm.
3. *Willingness of the people to change:* To bring about change in behaviour the extension worker's impact has to be restricted to initiate, motivate, and arouse interest on the part of the farmer to willingly participate and voluntarily change her/his practice, or adopt new skills. But new ideas should not be imposed or used to coerce people into compliance.

Extension is an applied science, which deals with the technical aspect of any development processes. Therefore, extension concepts and methods can be applied in the agricultural sector, cooperatives, health education, as well as in population education both in rural and urban areas. Hence, extension always receives its annexed names whenever it is applied in various development processes. For example, when it is applied in the agricultural sector it is to be called "Agricultural Extension". It is also called "Cooperative extension" when it is applied specifically in the cooperative development process.

Basic Principles of Agricultural Extension

Principles are tools to guide activities. Therefore, agricultural extension principles are used to guide/govern the activities of agricultural extension. Extension principles emanated from the very concept of extension dealing with the people. Human beings have needs, wants and desires.

Agricultural extension is a means to satisfy the needs, desires and wants of human beings. Agricultural extension can be used effectively in agricultural programmes, if it adheres to its basic principles. It can be used successfully to reach different groups of people with different messages in rural areas. The following are some of the principles of Agricultural extension:

Extension education should satisfy the needs of the learner, in providing knowledge and information. This means it should focus on the needs of the learners. The teaching learning process is very much influenced by the learner's needs. The perceived needs of the learners should be focused during the process.

Extension has been described as a system of out-of-school education for all rural/urban people. This explains why extension workers are regarded as teachers, for they constantly endeavor to teach people. Likewise, the extension worker (Cooperative promoter) should learn from the Adult learner as well. To be effective, the promoter must work together with the adult learner to help find solutions to the specific problems. By working with the adult as an equal partner in improving her/his situation (economic or otherwise), a trusting, interactive relationship may develop. If the extension worker approaches the adult learners as a listener, and helper, the client may be more willing to learn, and to improve her/his skills as a learner and decision maker.

It is important that the Adult should be included in the extension process at every stage. Only in this way can they be shown how the process of appraisal, evaluation, and innovation works and learn to solve their own problems. It is also important that the extension worker not to try to do all the work herself/himself, but should train local leaders to help so that her/his influence can be more widely spread.

The extension worker must be content with steady progress and avoid attempting to do too much to fast, for which he/she should stick to the following principles:

1. Direct efforts at clearly defined target groups. Who are we, or should we be addressing? (Groups by gender, age, etc.)
2. Tackle relevant problems. What are the target groups' main problems?
3. Make sure participants take an active part in educational events. How can they contribute to the educational process?
4. Pay attention to and respect people's own educational interests. To what extent do we allow adults to select from a range of educational possibilities; as opposed to confronting them with a set of formal curriculum approaches?
5. Develop an atmosphere of mutual trust and confidence between the learner and the communicator (teacher).

Importance of Agricultural Extension Services

Agricultural extension is accepted as the function of providing information and educational services to farmers about new technology. As a result, the role and mission of extension may vary widely.

Agricultural extension provides a service of communicating or introducing new ideas, techniques or materials to the farming community and communicates back the problems, experiences and needs of the farming community to the source (i.e., researchers, government agencies or educational institutions).

In general the role of agricultural extension activity is to promote the adoption of new technologies and practices such as the use of fertilizers, new variety seeds, seedbed preparations, methods of sawing, weed control, pest control and farm implements so as to enable the farmer at minimum cost, the production of sufficient food to feed the entire population; hence, attain better income and enjoy better living.

The role of agricultural extension is not only production-oriented, but also it may deal with family and home needs or the processing of farm products, as technology may not always deal with production.

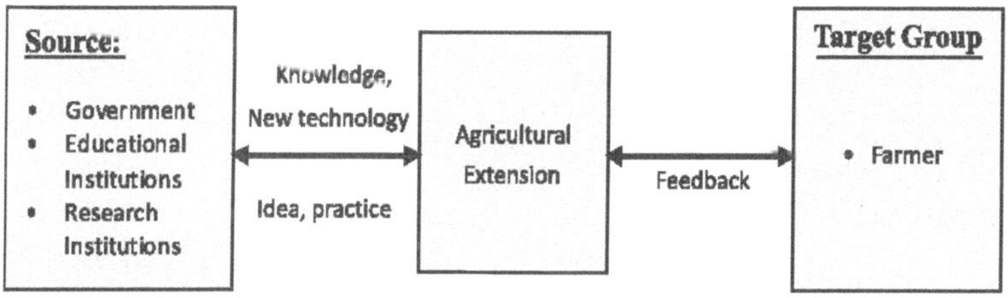

Fig. 5.1: **The role of Agricultural Extension**

TYPES AGRICULTURAL EXTENSION METHODS

Sources of Knowledge

Educationists recognized three sources of knowledge. These three sources of knowledge are discussed as follows:

1. *Informal education:* It is the life long process by which every person acquires and accumulates knowledge, skill, attitudes and insight from daily experiences and exposure to the environment.
2. *Formal education:* It is the chronologically graded and structured system of teaching at institutions from primary school to the University.
3. *Non-formal education:* It is an organized systematic teaching outside the formal system for groups of people with particular needs. It includes agricultural extension, adult literacy campaigns, and instruction in health (health extension), nutrition and family planning.

There are various educational methods or techniques available to the extension worker to choose from setting up learning situations to maximize the transfer of information and skills. The extension agent, extension worker at the village level in direct day to day contact with local farmers, actually teaches and informs farmers with various educational methods or techniques such as individual method, group method or mass method or media. Let us discuss in brief as under.

Individual Extension Method

In this method the extension worker interact on a one-to-one basis with the people. This approach helps the extension worker learns more about the people of the area; how they think, what their needs are and how they carryout their work. It also provides the local farming community to get to know the extension worker so that a personal relationship and mutual understanding between and the farmers can be established. This method allows the extension worker's credibility and integrity to flourish and strengthen. The disadvantage of using this method is — it requires high costs in terms of staff, time and travel, and small proportion of the target population can be reached.

This method can be applied by the techniques of individual extension on the farm where the discussion can take place in the farmer's fields, home, extension office or participatory method where the farmer is a vital partner in all decisions while the extension agent's role is to provide expertise and assistance to the farmer.

Group Extension Method

This is a form of teaching to groups and more common method in extension work than teaching individuals. This is because more farmers can be reached using group techniques than possible by individual methods. Group extension methods are useful, particularly when *time and staff* are limited. This method is effective in persuading farmers to try a new idea or practice. A group decision to try a new practice for instance may carry more weight or be likely to spread to other areas than a similar decision made by an individual. Therefore, group extension methods are used for advising and promoting the interest of a large number of farmers with a lesser cost and time saving.

The problems in group extension method is—it may take a long time to persuade a group of farmers to come to common decision, it is very difficult to relate new practices to the actual problems and situations of affective individual group and it is not easy to get a group together when needed. Some of the examples of group extension methods are demonstrations, field days, field trips, innovation meetings and group discussions.

Mass Extension Method

Mass extension method uses impersonal contacts rather than personal contacts as the individual and group extension methods to disseminate information and recommend changes in farming practices.

In mass extension method the techniques, that can be used, includes mass media, such as radio, television, films, exhibits, newspaper, magazines and other folk medias or live presentations, which includes plays, songs, puppet shows, story telling and other traditional form of entertainments; and media combination that is combining different methods since there is no best method rather what part each method can play in an extension programme should be considered.

MARKETING OF AGRICULTURAL INPUTS

Agricultural Inputs and Role of Cooperatives

Generally, agricultural can be classified as primitive agriculture and modern agriculture. Under primitive agriculture, farmers follow traditional methods of agriculture and they heavily depend on nature. Deep ploughing, rotation of crops, application of manure, crop protection measures, scientific marketing systems, etc. will not be followed under primitive agriculture.

Under modern agriculture, farmers use improved seeds, manure and chemical fertilizers, follow crop protection measures, go for deep ploughing, rotation of crops, intensive cultivation by way of taking more than one crop in a year on the same land. Assured irrigation facilities are developed under modern agricultural system. To face the natural calamities, the farmers are given crop and cattle insurance under modern agriculture. Here below, we can see the important inputs needed for agriculture.

Farmers are in need of the following inputs for their agriculture.

1. Improved seeds
2. Fertilizers (manure and chemical)
3. Pesticides
4. Fuel
5. Agricultural credit
6. Service inputs – marketing, processing, equipments, insurance, hiring of machineries

1. ***Improved Seeds***

   Improved seeds are one of the preconditions of modern agriculture and total agricultural production. Improved seeds developed in agricultural research centers have greater production potential and farmers must use them to increase their per hectare production. But there are certain issues relating to the availability of improved seeds.

   (a) *Cost of the improved seeds:* Compared to the traditional seeds collected in the farms by the farmers, the improved seeds are costlier. But the production will be higher than the traditional farm seeds.

   (b) *Timely availability:* The farmers must get the improved seeds well before the sowing season. So the cooperatives or other institutional agencies must take steps to provide the improved seeds even before the sowing season.

   (c) *Multiplication of seeds:* In certain cases, improved seeds may have to be imported from foreign countries. To multiply such seeds for the broader use of many farmers, it may take lot of time. This is one of the difficulties of improved seeds.

(d) *Finance required for the purchase:* As the improved seeds are costlier, the cooperatives or commercial banks must come forward to provide loans for the purchase of improved seeds. Otherwise, the farmers may find it difficult to apply such seeds to the farms.

2. *Fertilizers*

Farmers can use both manures and chemical fertilizers. Manure is obtained from cattle and it has become scarce due to the decreasing cattle population and the increased demand for fertilizers. So, the alternative for the farmers is to go for chemical fertilizers, which are manufactured in the factories. The tasks included in fertilizer are as follows:

(a) *Forecasting the demand by season, location, and type of fertilizer:* It is very difficult to forecast the exact demand for fertilizers. The use of fertilizer depends on the type of crop and the season on which they are going to cultivate such crops. Farmers may also be in need of various types of fertilizers like DAP, Urea, mixtures, etc. It is slightly difficult to assess the quantity of each fertilizer needed by the farmers.

(b) *Transport and distribution channels:* Chemical fertilizers are manufactured either in a particular country or imported by certain countries like Ethiopia. From the production center or the harbor terminal fertilizers are to be transported quickly and safely. Again, from the producer or importer, the fertilizers have to be distributed through the wholesalers, retailers, or cooperatives. An effective and efficient distribution channel alone can do good to the farmers. Cooperatives are the most suitable agencies to distribute fertilizers to the farmers quickly and at a reasonable price.

(c) *Credit needed to procure fertilizers:* Fertilizer, as an input is costlier. The farmers are in need of finance, which can be provided by cooperatives or commercial banks. Without such credit arrangements, small farmers and poor farmers cannot get fertilizer.

(d) *Advisory and demonstration services at the farm levels:* Farmers are in need of advisory services through extension workers about the type of fertilizer to be applied and at what time to be applied. It is the duty of the agricultural extension department to undertake such activities.

(e) *Cost of fertilizers:* When fertilizer is imported by private merchants, naturally the cost will be high. If fertilizer is imported by cooperatives and distributed through cooperatives, farmers get lot of benefits. For example, in Ethiopia, cooperative unions distribute the fertilizers below Birr 50 per quintal than the market price.

(f) *Effects relating to fertility of soil, environmental degradation:* Continuous use of chemical fertilizers would be harmful to the soil. So, the farmers must complement natural manure with chemical fertilizers to keep the fertility of the soil intact and to avoid harmful effects of chemical fertilizers.

3. *Pesticides/Herbicides*

Intensive agriculture led to the application of improved seeds and chemical fertilizers, which resulted in the multiplication of pest attack on crops. Farmers are in need of the application of chemical pesticides, fungicides, etc. Certain issues relating to the application of pesticides are as follows:

(a) *Higher cost of pesticides:* Like improved seeds and fertilizers, the cost of pesticides is high. So, the farmers must be provided with credit facilities.

(b) *Implements needed for its application:* To apply pesticides, instruments like sprayers and dusters are needed. These are costlier and an ordinary farmer cannot purchase it for use. So, facilities must be made by agencies like cooperatives to hire such instruments.

(c) *Harmful effects of chemical pesticides on crop:* Before applying the chemical pesticides, the farmers must consult the agricultural extension workers. Steps must be taken to avoid the harmful effects of chemical pesticides. Natural herbicides like neem powder can be substituted with chemical pesticides.

(d) *Environmental degradation:* Care should be taken that soil conditions are not spoiled by chemical pesticides. Chemical should not also pollute water and the environment. Too much chemicals may also not good for vegetables and fruits, which are consumed by human beings.

(e) *Immunity for the pest:* Continuous application of chemical pesticides may make the pest immune to such things, which may demand more dose of chemicals. Here, farmers have to be careful.

4. *Fuel*

Now-a-days farmers are in need of fuel like petrol and diesel to operate pump sets, tractor, harvester, etc. Electricity can supplement fuel in certain activities. Improved methods of agriculture demand assured irrigation facilities to the farmers. In remote areas, and in areas where canal or river irrigation is possible, farmers have to get the ground water through motor pump sets, for which fuel or electricity is needed.

5. *Agricultural Credit*

Agricultural credit is the basic input, which is called as prime mover for agricultural development. Through adequate credit farmers can purchase the needed inputs like seeds, fertilizer, pesticides, etc. A farmer is in need of three types of credit:

(a) *Short-term credit:* Such credit is needed for a period of 3 months – 15 months for the purchase of inputs, to meet farm expenses like the payment of wages, payment of electricity fees, taxes, etc.

(b) *Medium-term credit:* Such credit is needed for a period of 15 months – 5 years. Such credit is needed for the purchase of agricultural implements, purchase of cattle and milch animals, for the erection of pump sets, etc.

(c) *Long-term credit:* Long-term credit is needed for a period of 5 years – 15 to 20 years. It is needed to make permanent improvements on land like leveling of land, constructing bunds, fending the farmland, construction of farm shades, to dig wells and construct ponds for irrigation. It is also needed to purchase heavy agricultural implements like tractor, harvester, thresher, etc. Long-term credit is also needed to purchase new lands for extending farmlands.

6. *Service Inputs*

Farmers need of service inputs like marketing services, processing services, transport services, hiring of agricultural machineries, insurance, etc. Marketing is an important service needed for farmers. There are two types of marketing undertaken by marketing agencies, namely input marketing and output marketing. Input marketing denotes the supply of improved seeds, chemical fertilizers and pesticides to the farmers. Output marketing implies the selling of agricultural produces to the market. Cooperatives are considered to be the better agencies in providing marketing services to the farmers. Transport, grading, weighing, and storing are some of the services related to marketing services. Closely related to the marketing service is the processing service to be undertaken for the farmers. Through processing activity a raw agricultural commodity is converted into next form.

For example, conversion of wheat flour from raw wheat is a processing activity. Through processing activity value addition is given to the farmers, which fetches a higher price to their produce compared to the selling of raw agricultural produces. Hiring of agricultural machineries is one more service inputs needed by the farmers. As agricultural machineries are costlier, all farmers cannot purchase costly machineries. So, institutions like cooperatives can purchase such costly machineries and hire them to the farmers. Important agricultural machineries are tractor, sprayer, duster, harvester, etc. Insurance is another important service to be given to farmers. To protect the farmers' crop from natural calamities, crop insurance has been introduced. To protect the livestock, cattle insurance has been introduced. Such insurance services are undertaken by cooperatives, commercial banks, and insurance companies.

Agricultural inputs are at the heart of rural marketing and rural development. They support farm products, which is the source of income for a very large part of the rural population. Agricultural inputs are vehicles of modernization and rural change, as they are most of the time industrially processed, manufactured, packaged and branded products.

Agricultural inputs can be categorized into consumable and capital inputs. Consumable inputs include manure and fertilizer, seeds, insecticides pesticides, herbicides, etc. Among these fertilizers alone is the most important and widely used agricultural inputs. It is receiving continuous Government support for their promotion, market development because they contribute directly to food production. Capital inputs on other hand include; tractors, trailers, harvesters, thrashers, pump sets and other implements. They are so-called capital inputs because they require huge capital to own them.

The marketing of agricultural inputs differs from product marketing in terms of the nature of transaction; which includes participants, products, modalities and outcomes. The *participants* include producers, sellers, facilitators, regulators, buyers and consumers. Similarly the *products* are different as they are bulky, costly, used rarely, mostly being bought on credit and have derived demand. The *modalities* of a transaction, which include space, time, ownership utilities, roles and terms of various participants. The sales of inputs on credit and on subsidy are most important modalities of this market. Finally, the *outcome* of the transactions, in terms of satisfaction or lack of it has impact on subsequent transactions.

NATURE OF DEMAND

The agricultural inputs are b/n the consumer and industrial producers from the point of view of marketing mix (4Ps). The farmers do not use them like consumer products, but are used as per their demand. In these sense they are derived demand products. This means that demand for specific type of product or service depends greatly on the demand for another product or service for which it is used. The demand for fertilizer specially is a function of the demand for crops it helps to produce, that is, the demand for most farm supplies is derived from the demand for farm products. However, they are similar to consumer products as far as distribution and promotion aspects are concerned at these two are targeted at the farmer level. But so far as product and its price are concerned they are like industrial products as they are bulky, of higher cost and globally based. The inputs are also demanded not individually but as a *package*. Because one input decides the need for other inputs. This means that their demand is complementary to each other.

For example, a local hybrid seed will determine whether to use fertilizer or a pesticide in required quantity and quality. Further more, since the product is meant for the production process, sales of agricultural inputs are dependent on:

- The weather in season
- Cropping pattern changes
- Nature and health of the Crop
- Other facilities like Government price policy, subsidies, loans and physical facilities for the product.

The demand changes from season-to-season and month-to-month. Farmers and rural buyers are much open to spending especially if it helps to raise the level of their income. Farmers are skeptical about adopting products, which are *non-traditional* and *costly*. But if they are convinced with a demonstration in their fields, they feel much more comfortable with the products. Therefore such demonstrations have a great deal to play in the dissemination of new products and technologies. *Credit* also play a crucial role in agricultural input markets as most of the time the farmers resort to credit purchase of the inputs and intend to repay after harvest. Therefore, the *availability* and *cost of credit* for this purpose influences the quantity and quality of inputs used.

In agricultural input markets, there are serious problems of unbalanced usage due to under or over use of inputs, especially in chemical inputs; there is a wide disparity in their use across regions and high inefficiency in their usage. The soil in some regions has become acidic and caused the Agricultural output to decline sharply whether inputs are used correctly or not. These and other factors all together spoil the economics of inputs usage and therefore hurt the market for an input due to its bad image in terms of performance. Moreover in developing countries like Ethiopia various inputs like seeds, credit and equipment are provided through the moral development schemes and cooperatives. These affect the open market as they are at long rate. Also this put the private channels in to difficulty, as farmers start comparing the product and price with government and cooperatives supplied ones.

PROMOTIONAL MEDIA

Though a lot has changed in the market for inputs, still there are inexperienced users for various reasons. The opinion makers can be the progressive farmers in relatively long developed areas. The *input sellers (retailers)* are the promoters in the majority of the rural markets. *Extension agents* also play a significant role in the promotion of markets for agricultural inputs.

The promotional media helps agribusiness to inform ranchers and farmers about new and used equipments and chemicals as well as services so that they can sell more of the product or service. The promotion mix chosen by the agribusiness firm is usually a combination of advertising, personal selling, general publicity and a sales support programmes.

These promotional mixes with the particular reference to marketing of Agricultural inputs are discussed as follows:

Advertising

It is mass communication with potential customer usually through public communications media. Much advertising is initiated and sponsored by manufactures of agribusiness products. Some of this advertising is oriented toward the dealer or distributor to influence ordering and selling decisions. But much manufacturer sponsored advertising is aimed towards the final consumer in this case the farmer.

There is a wide variety of communications media ready to carry the agribusiness's message. Television is expensive and not widely used, since the facilities are not there as to our farmers. Radio is used more commonly, since it is less expensive and can target its farm audience by trying into agricultural programmes other medias include local radio stations, handbills and flyers sent directly to high potential customers, rural newspapers etc. Local, regional and national farm magazines are an important method of communication.

Sales Promotions

These are programmes and special offerings designed to attract interested customers into making a positive buying decision. There are varieties of tools and are often expensive but are felt by many to strongly influence customer decisions.

Some of these programmes are aimed directly at the final consumer, the farmer. Giving potential customers hats, caps, jackets, belt buckles, pens, note pads and other, all imprinted with company logo. Many suppliers use this kind of promotion. Other promotional programmes include educational-sales meetings sponsored by suppliers and retailers for farmers and ranchers; promoting the use of chemicals, hybrids, feeds, livestock breeds, and the like in meetings and seminars in providing technical information to producers; trade shows etc.

Personal Selling

At some points in the marketing process, a sale must be made and ownership of the product must be transferred. This requires human effort of some sort where the salesperson intentionally plays an important part in the promotion process by tailoring the promotion to individual needs.

Selling in agricultural supply industry can be selling to manufacturing and processing firms of fertilizers, pesticides, feed etc. Salespeople who sell to these firms usually deal with purchasing agents, and other highly specialized personnel. Thus the sales person to be more effective he has to be professional salesperson with agricultural background. The other type of selling is to selling distributors and wholesalers by the manufacturer in turn they sell to retailers or directly to farmers.

NATURE OF COMPETITION

In marketing, knowledge of competition is an important part of marketing strategy. Dominant firms are often vulnerable to competitive encroachments, thus these larger and more successful firms should not perpetuate the way of doing business that helped them become successful. In the agricultural supply industries there is an intense competition among firms providing agricultural chemicals to farmers with the introduction of free market economy. In our country private firms participating in this sector has increased and cooperative unions providing their members agricultural input is also increasing. However, they are yet to face intense competition from giant national and multinational private companies.

One simple but effective method for analyzing competition is completing a formal strength and weakness analysis for each competitor. This format simply lists key strengths and weakness of a competitor and then logically develops a strategy that capitalizes on the competitors' weakness.

Framework for Understanding the Market for Inputs

The experience of developing countries indicates that the growth of input markets is influenced by a large number of price as well as non-price factors. Based on the experience in India, China and sub-Saharan Africa including Ethiopia, a framework has been developed for understanding the market environment for agricultural inputs.

The major components of this framework are:

- Agronomic potential
- Agro-economic potential
- Effective demand
- Actual consumption

The market environment can be conceptualized as unfolding through the developments within and inter-relationship between these components.

1. *Agronomic potential*

Agricultural inputs can be considered to be primarily *yield saving* or *yield raising* units. Their basic usefulness to the farmer and their potential comes fundamentally from the quantity of yield they are able to raise or save. This gives the agronomic potential. Agricultural inputs may also help to improve quality. Inputs like pesticides also help to reduce the uncertainty or risk of obtaining good yields. Research and development are typically necessary for the certain of new agronomic potentials for inputs.

2. *Agro-Economic potential*

Inputs are typically expensive units. Unless the output is gained due to the use of inputs or lost due to its non-usage, which is of substantial value, farmers will not use inputs. The price of the output must be significantly high relative to the price of the input for the agronomic potential to be transformed in to agro-economic potential. Thus output markets and demands become important determinants of agro-economic potential.

3. *Effective demand*

Creation of an agro-economic potential may not be sufficient for real demand to exist in developing countries with subsistence agriculture. The farmers must know the economic opportunity and must exhibit entrepreneurship in exploiting this opportunity. Thus dissemination of information and extension work as well as company promotion become very important.

Poor infrastructure and lack of transportation services seriously affect the conversion of a good agro-economic potential in to effective demand, especially for small farmers. Since subsistence agriculture lacks cash and lags are involved in obtaining output, the provision of credit often becomes a very important factor.

4. *Actual Consumption*

Even when effective demand has been created, actual consumption may be strongly restricted unless there is:

- *Aggregate supply:* Adequate and reliable supply of the input is necessary either through production or import. This determined among other things, by the factors like investment in production, the investment environment, government policies, foreign exchange situation and other factors such as trade barriers and intellectual property rights protection.
- *Effective Distribution System:* A large effective distribution system should also be developed for catering to small farmers scattered over a large area at the right time. This is especially difficult in the early stages when the volumes are small.

Role of Cooperatives in Providing Agricultural Inputs in Ethiopia

There are various types of cooperatives that can provide various inputs needed by the farmers. The experience in developing countries have shown that one cooperative at the village level (multi-purpose cooperative) can provide all types of agricultural inputs and supplies to the farmers. But in developed countries separate cooperatives do individual services to the farmers. In Ethiopia, the primary cooperatives in collaboration with the cooperative unions distribute fertilizers and other inputs. To provide credit to the farmers, a beginning has been made by the SACCOs (Savings and Credit Cooperatives). The following are the observations of the cooperatives in Ethiopia in providing agricultural inputs to the farmers.

1. In Ethiopia primary cooperatives organized at kebele level are called by different names like primary cooperatives, producers' cooperatives, multi-purpose cooperatives, and service cooperatives. These primary cooperatives are primarily engaged in the distribution of fertilizers and the collection of dues for the cost of inputs. Unlike the other developing countries, primary cooperatives in Ethiopia are not providing agricultural credit to the farmers.
2. There are two types of primary cooperatives distributing inputs to the farmers. Under the first type, the primaries themselves procure the inputs in the market and supply them to the farmers. The second types of primary cooperatives are affiliated to the cooperative unions. The cooperative unions procure the inputs in the wholesale markets on behalf of the affiliated primary cooperatives and supply them to the farmers through the primary cooperatives.
3. The cooperative unions are bigger cooperative organizations meant for purchasing inputs to the farmers through the primaries and sell the agricultural produce on behalf of the farmers. During the year 2006, eight

cooperative unions in Oromiya region have got license from the ministry to import fertilizers directly from foreign countries. Through this process, they are able to sell the fertilizer Birr 50 per quintal lower than the market price. The cooperative unions procure the farm produces from the farmers and sell them for a good price on behalf of the primary cooperatives and farmers.

4. Some of the NGOs in Ethiopia are promoting and guiding the agricultural cooperatives as per the Cooperative Proclamation 147/1998. Such NGOs have organized special types of cooperatives called Seed Multiplication Cooperatives. These cooperatives are organized by the unemployed youth. They get improved seeds from the agricultural research stations through government quota. Afterwards, the seed multiplication cooperatives, through their members, multiply the seeds in the farms and sell them to the farmers. This process solves two purposes. The first one, the unemployed youth are able to get employment opportunity through seed multiplication and get good income. Secondly, the farmers are able to get improved seeds at a reasonable price without any shortage in these areas.

5. One of the preconditions for the efficient distribution of inputs is the transport system. Many primary cooperatives and cooperative unions are not having their own transport vehicles. So, they hire the transport vehicles from the private operators. The transport cost paid for such purposes is very high and the cooperatives can think of purchasing their own vehicles by getting financial help from the commercial banks.

Another precondition for the successful distribution of inputs is the storage system. A cooperative should have adequate stores or godowns to keep the stock safely and to distribute them throughout the season. Many cooperatives do not own their own stores and they hire private godowns or government godowns, which are costlier. So, such cooperatives must plan to construct their own stores.

Summary

- Agricultural Extension is the oldest extension established in 1944. Extension has been described as a system of out-of-school education for all rural/urban people. It is a systematically designed and planned activity, with its goal to bring about a lasting and permanent attitude changes among the clients. For common understanding we have to view extension as a process of helping people (farmers) make decisions by choosing from alternative solutions to their problems. Help implies that the learner's interest must be our starting point. In this case, *client-oriented* extension uses an educational approach, rather than providing simple services and/or advises.
- Extension has different meaning for different people. That is why different authors of Agricultural extension defined extension in different ways. However, the work of extension begins with the transfer or prevision of something with value.
- The role of Agricultural extension service is communicating or introducing new ideas, techniques or materials to the farming community and communicates back the problems, experiences and needs of the farming community to the source (i.e., researchers, government agencies or educational institutions).
- Among the three common methods of extension, group extension method is the most common in Ethiopia, as it is time-saving, cost-effective and require relatively few workforce than the individual method of extension.
- Agricultural inputs are at the heart of rural marketing and rural development. Agricultural inputs are vehicles of modernization and rural change, as they are most of the time industrially processed, manufactured, packaged and branded products.
- The rural marketing of agricultural inputs as activity differs from agricultural products marketing in terms of the nature of transaction; which includes participants,

products, modalities and outcomes. Agricultural inputs can be categorized in to consumable and capital inputs. Consumable inputs include manure and fertilizer, seeds, insecticides, and pesticides. Capital inputs include tractors, trailers, harvesters and threshers, pump sets, and other implements. The inputs are demanded not individually but as a package. Because one input decides the need for other inputs. This implies that their demand is complementary to each other.

- The promotional media helps agribusiness to inform ranchers and farmers about new and used equipments and chemicals as well as services so that they can sell more of the product or service. The promotion mix chosen by the agribusiness firm is usually a combination of advertising, personal selling, general publicity and a sales support programmes.
- In our country private firms participating in this sector has increased and cooperative unions providing their members agricultural input is also increasing. However, they are yet to face intense competition from giant national and multinational private companies.
- The experience of developing countries indicates that the growth of input markets is influenced by a large number of price as well as non-price factors. Based on this experience a framework has been developed for understanding the market environment for agricultural inputs. The major components of this framework are: agronomic potential, agro-economic potential, effective demand and actual consumption.

Self-Learning Activity

Try to answer the following questions on your own:

1. Explain basic principles of agricultural extension.
2. Compare individual and group extension methods.
3. What is the role of cooperatives in supplying agricultural inputs?

6

Agricultural Marketing and Processing

AGRICULTURAL PROCUREMENT AND PROCESSING SERVICES

The demand for supply is increasing as the farmer is becoming dependent on supply. Today farmers producers' are in need of services. These are services related to procurement, processing and preservation services and facilitating services or facilitating marketing functions. To meet this demand it requires an efficient and economic supply system. The private trader, especially in developing countries, has often proved unable to carry out this task adequately. Apart from charging unjustifiable high margins on the supplies, he usually does not have technical knowledge or time for the extension work, which should accompany the selling of farming supplies. As an alternative, many farmers turn to cooperative society as their sources of supply. Cooperatives carry a wide variety of supplies and services related to farm commodity production. Services provided by the typical purchasing or farm supply cooperatives vary somewhat according to the area it serves. Some carry a relatively limited line of supplies related to members needs. Examples of supplies and services provided include veterinary supplies like syringes, dehorners, vaccinating services; chemicals like herbicides, insecticides, fungicides, fertilizer and machinery like tractors, planters, sprayers, harvesters, irrigation equipment, spare parts; hand tools—hammers, hoes, shovels, sickles and services of plowing, planting, spraying, fertilizing, harvesting etc.

The objective of such a cooperative activity should be:

- To keep the prices of farming supplies at reasonable level by exercising collective bargaining power based on bulk buying; by shortening the supply lines through direct purchase from factories or importers or through its own production and by efficient handling to avoid loses and waste.
- To supply goods and services of a type and quality which are to be the best advantage of the farmer.

AGRICULTURAL PROCUREMENT SERVICES

Cooperative Buying Rings

It is a simple way of cooperative agricultural supply. The rings operate by collective orders from members, negotiating the purchase, supervising distribution and collecting payment.

The small amount of administrative work can be done by voluntary unpaid committee members. There is no paid staff and fixed assets such as storage space as the supply distributed directly from car or committeeman's farm on the arrival of order truck load. They are really only suitable for certain bulk supplies such as fertilizer.

Purchasing cooperatives

They differ from the buying rings in that they have to keep a stock of assorted supplies and that they undertake a considerably higher risks. Before the society order supplies it has to find out what to buy, when and how much to buy and where to buy.

Assortment

At initial stage the type of supply to be provided will usually be discussed at the general meeting. It is advisable for the society to limit itself to the more basic farming supplies. E.g. artificial fertilizer, selected seed etc. At a later stage the planning of the assortment is usually more or less left to the decision of the committee and the manager, and only the outline is decided at the general meeting.

The points to be considered in planning the assortment are:

- The demand from the farmers, assessed from informative talks with the members and, as time goes on, increasingly from experiences gained in the previous seasons using sales records.
- The possible changes in demand during the coming season.
- The assortment of farming supplies on the market, taking into consideration their relative quality and prices.
- The assortment offered by firms, which compete with the society in or near its area of operation.
- Any side effects arising from the introduction of new lines. It must be considered that the sale of certain farming supplies is only possible if the appropriate facilities or services provided. For instance sale of farming machinery is usually only possible if an efficient repair and maintenance services can be arranged.

Order size and time

In deciding the quantity to be ordered, the society will have to estimate first the total demand for the coming period, which can be made some kind of advance order system. Each member will be discussed the amount of supplies needed, and collect the orders. The orders can be 'loose', i.e. the farmer has no obligation to buy, or 'binding'. The latter type is more desirable as the risk is kept at a minimum.

At latter years the estimate of the total future demand will be largely based on past experience, i.e. the sales during previous periods and the average increase or decrease in sales during the year.

After determining the total demand the order size i.e. whether the order or delivery should be in one lot or in several successive deliveries is influenced by the following factor.

- The period over which the demand stretches compared with the delivery schedules of the supplier or the possibility of collecting.
- The available storage spaces.
- The available capital to pay for the supplies.

If these factors allow the choice between one or several lots, the optimum order size will be determined by the comparative costs. The increased costs of bulk buying caused by an increased demand for storage space and capital and the higher risk must be compared with the increase in administrative, handling and purchase costs combined with buying in small lots.

The timing of the order should be so that the supplier has sufficient time to arrange delivery before the demand arises or, in the case of a continuous demand, before the stock on hand runs out.

Source of Supply

The question where to buy requires careful study and a composition of various supply possibilities.

The offers received should be compared with respect to:

- The quoted price, terms of delivery and trade discount.
- The terms of payment, i.e. the period of credit extended to the society and the alternative cash discount offered.
- The delivery date or schedule, i.e. the time it would take for the society to receive the goods.
- The reputation and especially, the reliability of the supplier.

CHALLENGES FOR GRAIN MARKETING SYSTEMS

Depot network and distribution of production problems arise because crop production is rarely evenly distributed across a country. In most countries cereals production is concentrated in one or two regions of the country, and the remainder are cereals deficit areas. In these circumstances it usually becomes rational and necessary for the government agency handling grain distribution, where there is one, to construct intake depots in the producing region(s), and storage depots in the major consumption areas. But in most instances, post-independent governments in some of these countries adopted rural income policies that made it mandatory for the whole country to be provided with government agency depots within short distances of every producer. The aim was to overcome political, social and economic injustices of the past. It was a policy which was also pursued in the hope that smallholder farmers would be attracted into the cash economy. In the end, this huge investment in infrastructure was economically unsustainable and most developing countries are now locating storage facilities on the basis of economic efficiency.

Excess stock problems tend to develop because of relatively high producer prices which the governments of the countries concerned establish in order to compensate farmers whose cost for production are high. Unfortunately, these systematic increases in the producer prices usually bring them to levels that are incompatible with international supply and demand conditions. To reduce the effect of these high producer prices some governments in LDCs introduced artificial exchange rates that later did more harm than good to the export economy of these countries. In addition, local demand was low, being limited to only urban demand, for human consumption, and for livestock feed production in rural areas.

Fluctuating grain supply problem results from the crop's susceptibility to weather conditions, which determine the level of harvest and, therefore, the export market supply. With each country's domestic demand often varying along with the weather, LDC countries have been known to rapidly move from a surplus to a deficit situation. In a country with high import parity and low export parity prices, the increased risk of stockpiling seems to lower the real cost of storing the excess stocks and so causes government to become indifferent toward streamlining supply with demand requirements. Low levels of intra-regional trade between developing countries is explained by subsidies paid to producers. This masks any competitive advantage in grain production that growers in one country may have over those in neighbouring countries. Where there is intra-regional trade in grains, between developing countries it is most often based on periodic shortages arising from drought civil strife. As such, export demand is usually short-lived and often financed by donor agencies, and the exporting country cannot make any long term plans to develop the trade.

PRODUCT PROCESSING AND PRESERVATION

Food Processing and Preservation is a branch of manufacturing that transforms raw animal, vegetable, or marine materials into tasty, nutritious, and safe food products. The industry has its roots in ancient times, as humans have always needed to obtain food and store a portion for later use. Prehistoric humans may have dried fruits in the sun and stored meat in cold areas, such as caves. The modern food processing and preservation industry was born in 1809, when French chef and inventor Nicolas Appert, searching for a better way to provide food for Napoleon's army, devised a method for sterilizing food in tightly sealed glass bottles.

Today a wide variety of methods are available to maintain and enhance the appearance and taste of food. Food processing and preservation methods also create products that are convenient for consumers, such as products that are ready to eat or require minimal preparation and cooking. Combining these methods with modern distribution networks makes seasonal crops available year-round in grocery stores all over the world.

PROCESSING AND PRESERVATION SERVICES

Product processing encompasses all the steps that product goes through from the time it is harvested to the time it arrives on supermarket shelves. At simplest, processing may involve only picking, sorting, and washing fruits and vegetables before they are sent to market. Some processing methods convert raw materials into a different form or change the nature of the product, as in the manufacture of sugar from sugar beets or sugar cane, oil from corn or olives, or cheese from milk. Processing may also involve an extremely complex set of techniques and ingredients to create ready-to-eat convenience foods.

Most agricultural produce is not in a form suitable for direct delivery to the consumer when it is first harvested. Rather it needs to be changed in some way before it can be used. Kohls and Uhl observe that:

"The processing function is sometimes not included in a list of marketing functions because it is essentially a form changing activity".

However, it is for this very reason that processing ought to be included as a marketing function. The form changing activity is one of that adds value to the product. Changing green coffee beans into roasted beans, cassava into gari or livestock feed, full fruit bunches into palm oil or sugarcane into gur increases the value of the product because the converted product has greater utility to the buyer. How the form of produce is to be changed and the method to be used in bringing about such changes are marketing decisions. For example, some years ago when Ethiopia was looking to expand its tea business, a prototype manufacturing plant was established. The plant was capable of curing the tea and packing it in individual tea bags. At that point, tests were undertaken in which the product was compared with others already on the market. The results were encouraging. However, in the course of the marketing research, it was also discovered that ninety per cent of the black tea consumed is blended and not the pure variety placed in tea bags by the

Ethiopians. By going past the point of changing green leaf into high quality black tea, the Ethiopians were entering a nice market which is not what they intended at all. Timely marketing research would have directed Ethiopia to stop the form changing activity short of bagging since, at that time, Ethiopia did not have the acreage of tea, nor the resources, to develop a tea blending facility of its own. In the same way, a producer of fresh fruits may have pulping and/or canning facilities but if potential buyers want the flexibility of using the fruits in a variety of ways, then these stages of processing serve to reduce utility and value, rather than increasing them.

Of course, processing is not the only way of adding value to a product. Storing products until such times, as they are needed adds utility and therefore adds value. Similarly, transporting commodities to purchasing points convenient to the consumer adds value. In short, any action which increases the utility of the good or service to prospective buyers also adds value to that product or service.

SIGNIFICANCE OF AGRO-BASED INDUSTRIES

Agro-based industries are mainly engaged in transforming the raw materials into a finished or semi-finished form. Processing of agricultural produce is one of the important functions of agriculture, which provides value addition to the agricultural products. Processing implies the transformation of products from their non-usable form to usable form. Processing increases the value of the products and makes it possible to retain them for a longer period. It ensures their ready supply throughout the year and thus helps the stabilization of the price. In developing countries, processing is of immense advantage since it helps agriculture a profitable profession. But the individual farmer cannot undertake it owing to limited resources, in terms of finance, technical skill, and limited marketable surplus. Consequently, processing is undertaken by middleman in the private sector, who takes away the profit from the farmers. So, it is ideal to organize agro-based processing cooperatives by the farmers.

Processing can be done either by indigenous methods or by mechanical power. The former method can be of advantage only in those areas where unemployment or underemployment is rampant. But, in areas where there is shortage of manpower and where the problem is one of reducing the cost, processing by mechanical power would be economical.

In Ethiopia, our chief problem is to create employment opportunities for the rural people. It is therefore, necessary that labor-intensive methods are to be adopted for processing of agricultural produce. Hence, indigenous methods may be adopted in rural areas while mechanical power may be employed in urban areas. Again commodities, which are meant chiefly for export, may be processed with the help of mechanical appliances.

Agro-Processing cooperatives have been flourishing in the field of sugar, rice, fruit processing etc. These cooperatives involves huge amount of capital and managerial expertise. Processing cooperatives like the sugar cooperatives have become the growth centers and stimulate the growth of rural economy.

Processing of agricultural commodities can take the following two forms:

1. A change in the appearance or substance of the produce achieved by extracting, pressing, separating, maturing and similar transformations carried out by dairy industries, coffee industries, cotton ginneries, grain and oil mills, and fruit juice factories.
2. An increase in the durability by canning, chilling, freezing, dehydrating, smoking, salting, or some other form of preservation.

Circumstance that Favour the Organization of Agro-based Industries

1. *Perishable nature:* Agricultural commodities are perishable in nature. They should be sold or processed immediately.

By processing, the life of such goods is extended. The necessity for processing at cooperative level can arise particularly in the marketing of perishable produces if the distance to the market requires long periods of transit.

2. *Over supply:* Some of the commodities, like vegetables, fruits, and milk will have oversupply during certain seasons. During such periods, the surplus could be processed. If seasonable oversupply creates the need for an extended storage period, or if the available storage facilities cannot cope with current deliveries.
3. *Middlemen exploitation:* In every field of agricultural activities, middlemen are there. They are prevalent in agricultural credit, agricultural marketing, agricultural processing, and other agricultural activities. Efforts to free the farmers from the exploitation of middlemen is inevitable in agriculture. The monopoly of the middlemen could be broken by the cooperatives.
4. *Stabilized income for the farmers:* Agricultural production is seasonal in nature and farmers get income only during the harvest. Cooperative processing can attempt to stabilize the income of the farmers both in the short run and long run.
5. *Perishable products:* By joint processing through cooperatives, perishable products like milk, meat, fruits, vegetables and fish can be converted into higher value form and can save the producers from spoilage and low price.
6. *Job creation:* Cooperative processing creates full employment opportunity both to the members and the member's family. In the factory, lot of skilled and unskilled workers can be given employment.

Factors for the Organization of Agro-based Industries

Lots of procedural activities are involved in establishing agro-based industries. Their success, to a greater extent depends on nature. If monsoon fails or crop is damaged, it affects these units directly. Before organizing a agro-based unit the following aspects must be considered.

1. The place where the unit is to be organized must be nearer to the raw material area. Processing cooperatives can be organized at woreda level and the location can be in the center of the raw material area.

2. The size of the unit, capital involved and machineries needed must be decided. These things could be decided by the members and the number of producers promoting the cooperatives as members. Members should contribute to the working capital and the long-term capital can be borrowed from financial institutions.

3. A feasibility study must be conducted. The study must assess:

   (a) The suitability of the product for processing and the economic prospects of the industry

   (b) The price of raw material and the selling price of the product

   (c) The size and location of the industry

   (d) The cost of the project and the unit cost (fixed capital and working capital)

   (e) The process of production

   (f) Assurance of continuous supply of raw material

   (g) Manpower needs

   (h) Transport arrangements

   (i) Distribution arrangements

   (j) Capacity unitization

   (k) Profitability of the investment

4. The help of the promotional agencies for finance, marketing, technical assistance, etc. Banking institutions must help the processing cooperatives by way of short-term and long-term loans. The capital that could be

mobilized from the members can be used as short-term/ working capital. The long-term loan can be issued by specialized institutions like industrial banks, government agencies, etc. For marketing or selling the finished products cooperative processing can link with consumer cooperatives and cooperative supermarkets.

5. The technology to be used for the agro-based unit. There are three types of technologies, namely indigenous technology, intermediate technology, and latest technology. Cooperative processing units can go for intermediate technology or latest technology. But latest technology is costlier.
6. A part of the financial needs of the unit must be met from the members out of their share capital contribution. The rest of the finance can be arranged through financial institutions.
7. The type of personnel needed, both skilled and unskilled must be decided. A permanent recruiting system, training system, and welfare system must be planned.
8. The gestation period of the unit is another consideration. Gestation period means the time taken to install the machineries and start production. The time schedule to erect the unit must be strictly followed. Any delay in erecting the machines and starting the working will lead to additional expenditure.
9. Getting other infrastructure facilities like, power, transport, communication, finance, machineries, etc. must be considered. It is the duty of the federal and regional governments to provide the above infrastructure facilities. Before starting a processing unit, the promoters must weigh these facilities.
10. Government regulations, licensing policies, tax concessions, subsidies, market regulations, etc. must be made properly. In developing countries governments are giving concessions to cooperatives in licensing, marketing, price regulations, etc.

IMPORTANCE OF AGRO-BASED INDUSTRIES

Agro-based industries are organized mainly using agricultural raw materials. The popular agricultural raw materials are cotton, sugar cane, tobacco, bamboo, food grains like teff, wheat, barley, maize, etc. Fruits and vegetables can also be included because they are to be converted into fruit juices, tinned fruits, etc. Dairy industry can also be brought, because milk is basically an agriculture-oriented production. All the above said products are available in plenty in Ethiopia and there is enormous scope to organize small scale and big industries in these areas.

The following are the importance of agro-based industries, especially an agriculture based country like Ethiopia:

1. *Base for rural industrialization:* Agro-based industries, besides strengthening the function of agricultural credit and marketing system, will provide a wide base for rural industrialization. It has been seen that wherever the agro-industries have been in the rural areas, the rural economy gets immediately transformed and immensely strengthened. Larger surpluses become available for further investment and larger inputs make for technical and economic advance in both agricultural and industry.
2. *Socio-Economic change:* Agro-based industries have proved to be an effective instrument of socio-economic change of the areas in which they are located. They have created not only economic opportunities, but have helped in building a class of entrepreneurs from amongst ordinary farmers. Besides, they accelerates the rate of capital formation in agriculture both at the production and processing stages.
3. *Release from exploitation:* They free the farmers from the exploitation by dealers, processors and middlemen. This is due to the fact that they get good price to their produces.

4. *Stability of Income:* Agro-based industries provide a stable income to the farmers. The commodities they produce will have ever growing demand for such industries and the farmers get benefited by way of continued income.
5. *Improving Bargaining Power:* By joint processing through co-operatives of perishable produce like milk, meat, fruit, vegetables and fish, the producers can improve their negotiating position, a better price for their produce.
6. *Value Addition:* Agro-based industries ensured that the added value accrued to the member-producers, if such units are organized in cooperatives, where it would otherwise have passed into the hands of the various owners of the processing companies.
7. *Job Creation:* Agro-based industries can create direct employment opportunities to the villagers around the area of its location. Indirectly they can create employment opportunities by encouraging ancillary and allied industries.

TYPES OF AGRO-BASED INDUSTRIES

Classification of Agro-based Industries

Agro-based industries use agriculture and agriculture related commodities as raw materials. Such commodities are food grains, fruits, milk or dairying, commercial crops like sugarcane, tea and coffee, livestock products like meat and egg.

Such classifications are as follows:

1. **Food grains based**

   Many of the food grains like paddy, wheat,barley,teff and maize become raw material for processing industries. These produces are converted into powder form or semi finished commodities. The end products are biscuits, chocolate, glucose, alcohol etc.

2. **Fruits based**

   Fruits like banana, apple, orange, avacad etc. have ample scope to be processed in the form of cut fruits, juices, jam and fruit mixtures. During surplus production periods such products can be converted into above forms.

3. **Dairy products**

   Dairy products like milk, butter cheese etc. have enormous scope for reproduction or recon version into many other products like ice cream, ghee, cholate, condenced baby food etc.

4. **Commercial crops**

   Commercial crops like sugarcane, tea, coffee, coco, cotton, tobacco etc. have larger scope for processing. Cotton industry occupies a greater place in many countries in providing employment and export opportunities. Sugarcane forms the major raw material for sugar. Tea and coffee form another major form for processing and commercial production.

5. **Livestock products**

   Livestock provide good scope for processing industries. Meat industry can provide employment as well as export scope. Leather industry can promote shoe manufacturing, bag and leather coat manufacturing products. Likewise, egg becomes an important livestock product. Surplus egg can be powdered and has export potential. It can be preserved for a long period.

TYPES OF AGRO-BASED PRODUCTS

Above discussion gives a clear picture of various agro-based industries. The following discussion gives a picture of various forms of agro-based products.

I. Grain Processing

Grain processing is the most important activity from the final consumer's stand point within the marketing chain of the crop. Grain, for human consumption, is usually milled into flour or meal. Usually two types of maize flour are processed in each country, namely: the refined, white and sifted (powdery) flour produced by industrial roller mills and the unrefined and coloured maize meal produced by hammer-mills. The highly refined grade of meal is generally consumed by urban dwellers, while the hammer-mill grain meal is a low-grade "whole maize meal" favoured by rural consumers and the urban poor.

In many countries, the milling industry is highly concentrated, usually with one major company controlling over eighty per cent of the maize mill trade. For example, in Kenya, maize milling is controlled by the Mercat Group of Companies (Unga Ltd, etc) (90%): while in Malawi, it is Gramil, a subsidiary of Armarc which processes eighty-three per cent of the maize in that country. In Tanzania, the National Milling Corporation, (NMC) handled about eighty-five per cent of all maize milled before it fell into financial difficulties in the early 1990s and was allowed to go out of business; in Zimbabwe it is the National Foods which controls eighty per cent of maize milling in the country until progressive liberalization of the market increased the level of competition during the first five years of the 1990s. Grains can also undergo secondary processing and be converted into more sophisticated products such as baked foods, breakfast cereals, baby foods, cooking oils, starches, sugars etc. A considerable amount of grain is also converted to animal feed. Due to this versatility in end-use, the marketing chain for grains tend to be long and complex.

II. Food Preservation

Food preservation refers specifically to the processing techniques that are used to keep food from spoiling. Spoilage is any change that makes food unfit for consumption, and includes chemical and physical changes, such as bruising and browning; infestation by insects or other pests; or growth of micro-organisms, such as bacteria, yeast, and molds.

Some food preservation techniques destroy enzymes, proteins that are present in all raw foods, which are responsible for the chemical and physical changes that naturally occur after harvesting. Food preservation techniques also help eliminate the moisture or temperature conditions that are favorable for the growth of micro-organisms. As they multiply and grow, micro-organisms are capable of causing food-borne illness. They also break down foods, producing unpleasant changes in taste, texture, and appearance-changes that we recognize as spoilage. Although people have known about spoilage and some preservation methods to prevent it for centuries, it was only in 1857 that French chemist Louis Pasteur demonstrated the role of micro-organisms in the process.

Curing

Curing is one of the oldest forms of food preservation. It is used to preserve meat and fish, yielding common products such as bacon, ham, frankfurters, and corned beef. Curing involves adding some combination of salt, sugar, spices, vinegar, or sodium nitrite to animal foods. Smoking, a flavoring technique and preservation method, is another ancient technique that is commonly used with curing. Smoking involves cooking meat or fish very slowly over a low wood fire. Curing and smoking preserve food by binding or removing water so that it is not available for the growth of micro-organisms. These methods impart a distinctive colour and flavor to food and, in some cases, eliminate the need for refrigeration. Some studies, however, show that curing agents such as sodium nitrite may combine with other chemicals to form cancer-causing nitro amines. In addition, cured products tend to be very salty, and the sodium in salty foods has been linked to high blood pressure. Smoked meats and fish may contain toxic and even carcinogenic compounds that they absorb from wood smoke.

Drying

Drying has been used to preserve food by cultures throughout the world since prehistoric times, when people learned that dried foods, for example, fruits left out in the sun, remain wholesome for long periods. In modern times, the dried foods industry greatly expanded after World War II (1939-45) but remains restricted to certain foods, including milk, soup, eggs, fruits, yeast, some meats, and instant coffee, that are particularly suited to the process. Three basic methods of drying are used today: *sun drying*, a traditional method in which foods dry naturally in the sun; *hot air drying*, in which foods are exposed to a blast of hot air; and *freeze-drying*, in which frozen food is placed in a vacuum chamber to draw out the water. Removing the water preserves food because micro-organisms need water to grow and food enzymes cannot work without a watery environment. Removing the water also decreases the weight and volume of foods, thereby reducing transportation and storage costs. However, dried foods may be less convenient for consumers because most must be rehydrated before consumption. In addition, most dried foods only reabsorb about two-thirds of their original water content, leaving the rehydrated product with a tougher, chewier texture than the original. Some scientists and consumer groups have raised concerns about the sulfites commonly added to fruits before drying to prevent browning. These chemicals may cause severe allergic reactions in people with asthma or other people sensitive to the chemicals.

In *freeze-drying*, frozen food is placed in a special vacuum cabinet. There, water escapes from the food by sublimation, a process in which ice changes from a solid directly to a vapor without first becoming a liquid. Freeze-dried foods retain their original flavor, texture, and nutrients upon rehydration but must be packaged in moisture-proof, hermetically sealed containers. Freeze-drying is an expensive process used for such products as instant coffee, dried soup mixes, strawberries, mushrooms, and shrimp.

Canning

Canning is used to preserve a wide variety of foods, including soups, sauces, fruits, vegetables, juices, meats, fish, and some dairy products. Canning preserves food by heating it in airtight, vacuum-sealed containers. The can is filled with food, and air is pumped out of the space remaining at the top of the can to form a vacuum. The container is sealed, heated in a cooker called a retort, and then cooled to prevent overcooking of the food inside. This process removes oxygen, destroys enzymes involved in food spoilage, and kills most micro-organisms that may be present in the food.

Canned foods are popular because they are already partially prepared and cooked, can be stored without refrigeration for long periods, and are generally low in cost. However, because of the high temperatures required for sterilization, canning affects the colour, texture, flavor, and nutrient content of foods. Fat-soluble vitamins and minerals are barely affected by heat processing, but water-soluble vitamins, especially thiamine, riboflavin, and vitamin C, can leach into canning or cooking water that may later be thrown away during preparation. Up to half of the original content of water-soluble vitamins in a canned product can be lost in this way. Rapid, high-temperature processes generally conserve nutrient content best, as every 4.4°C (18°F) rise in processing temperature yields approximately a ten-fold increase in microbial destruction, with little additional nutrient loss.

Additives

Food additives are chemicals that are added to food in small amounts. Direct additives are added deliberately during processing to make food look and taste better, maintain or improve nutritive value, maintain freshness, and help in processing or preparation. Some additives help preserve food by preventing or slowing chemical changes and the growth of micro-organisms in food. As many as 3000 substances are approved by the Food and Drug Administration (FDA) for use as direct additives. An additional 10,000 substances are present in foods as indirect additives. These substances enter food incidentally during handling or from processing equipment or packaging.

Food additives have been used for thousands of years. The salts and other chemicals used in curing are additives, and before the advent of canning and mechanical refrigeration, chemical additives were the only means of preservation available. Additives were not limited to use as preservatives, however, people in ancient Rome added certain chemicals to wine and cooked vegetables to improve the colour of these foods. Other examples of additives that have been used since ancient times include yeast and baking powder used as leavening in baked goods.

In the 20th century, advances in the knowledge of chemistry have greatly expanded the number of additives that are used in foods. Such recent additions to the ranks of food additives include artificial sweeteners, such as aspartame and saccharin; fat replacements, such as simplesse; and colours, such as FD & C yellow No. 5, which is used in beverages, ice cream, cereals, and other foods.

The development of new chemical additives has also played an enormous role in the growth of convenience foods. Additives that help ensure the quality of convenience foods include anti-caking agents, such as calcium silicate and magnesium stearate, to prevent lumps in dry mixes; humectants, such as glycerol, propylene glycol, and sorbitol, to help retain moisture in breads and cakes; emulsifiers, such as egg yolk, lecithin, and monoglycerides, which bind oil and water to improve the uniformity and smoothness of foods; and stabilizers and thickeners, such as guar gum, carrageenan, and gelatin.

As the use of food additives has grown, so has public concern about the type and amount of these additives and their potential to cause cancer or other illnesses in human beings. Some studies have suggested that saccharin, nitrites, and other additives may cause cancer, but these results remain controversial. At the same time, some additives may actually provide a health benefit. For example, the vitamins used to fortify foods such as bread and milk are additives.

Freezing and Refrigeration

Low-temperature storage as a preservation method probably began when prehistoric humans stored meat and other foods in ice caves. However, mechanical refrigeration and large-scale freezing are relatively recent innovations. Mechanical refrigeration was pioneered by American inventor John Gorrie in 1842, but a mechanical refrigeration system suitable for widespread commercial use was not developed until the 1870s. American inventor Clarence Birdseye developed procedures, equipment, and packaging for quick-freezing in the 1920s, and in 1953 frozen TV dinners were introduced by C. A. Swanson and Sons.

Storage at low temperature slows many of the enzymatic reactions involved in spoilage and reduces the growth rate of microorganisms (though it does not kill them). To minimize microbial growth, refrigerators should be kept at 0° to 4°C (32° to 40°F) and freezers at or below 0°C (32°F). Refrigeration is advantageous because it does not cause chemical or physical changes to food. Freezing allows foods to be stored for longer periods than refrigeration because it inhibits enzyme activity and microbial growth to a greater degree. The greatest disadvantage of freezing is that the water in food expands and forms ice crystals. The ice crystal formation disrupts the structure of plant and animal cells, giving frozen food a softer texture after thawing. Newer technologies in which freezing occurs more rapidly help minimize this problem: faster freezing means that smaller ice crystals form, resulting in less damage to cells.

Foods that should be refrigerated include meat, fish, eggs, milk, some fruits, and some vegetables. Many of these foods can also be frozen. Frozen produce is often high in quality and can rival the flavor of fresh. In many cases, produce frozen and stored under proper conditions contains more nutrients than produce picked unripened and allowed to mature during transportation. Briefly cooking vegetables in boiling water before freezing, a process known as blanching, inactivates enzymes altogether and reduces discoloration and nutrient loss.

Controlled Atmosphere Storage

Fruits and vegetables are sometimes stored in sealed warehouses where temperature and humidity are closely controlled, and perhaps most importantly, the composition of gases in the atmosphere is altered to minimize spoilage. Usually, the concentration of oxygen is reduced, the concentration of carbon dioxide is increased, and ethylene, a gas naturally produced by plants that accelerates ripening, is removed from the atmosphere. This controlled environment helps slow the enzymatic reactions that eventually lead to decomposition and decay, and may increase the time that produce can be stored by several months. Ripening rooms, in which ethylene gas is added to the atmosphere, also help produce higher quality fruits and vegetables. This technology enables produce to be picked before it is ripe, for easier handling, and then ripened quickly and uniformly under controlled conditions.

Aseptic Packaging

Aseptic packaging is now commonly used for packaging milk and juice. Like canning, aseptic packaging involves heat sterilization of food, but unlike canning, the package and food are sterilized separately. Food can be sterilized more rapidly and at lower temperatures in aseptic packaging than in canning, allowing the food to retain more nutrients and better flavor. Containers are sterilized with hydrogen peroxide rather than with heat, permitting the use of plastic bags and foil-lined cartons, which would be destroyed by heat sterilization. These containers cost less than the metal and glass containers used in canning and also weigh less, reducing transport costs. Aseptically packaged foods will keep without refrigeration for long periods of time, perhaps even years. They are growing in popularity because of their low cost, good taste and nutrition, and convenience.

Irradiation

Irradiation is a process in which food is passed through a chamber where it is exposed to gamma rays or X rays. These high-energy rays are strong enough to break chemical bonds, destroy cell walls and cell membranes, and break down deoxyribonucleic acid (DNA), the substance that carries genetic information in all cells. Irradiation kills most bacteria, molds, and insects that may contaminate food. Irradiation also delays the ripening of fruits and sprouting of vegetables, permitting produce to be stored for longer periods of time. Because irradiation involves minimal heating, it has very little effect on the taste, texture, and nutritive value of food.

The FDA first approved irradiation for use on wheat and wheat flour in 1963, and later approved its use on white potatoes, spices, pork, some fresh produce (onions, tomatoes, mushrooms, and strawberries), and poultry. In 1997, in response to several food-borne illness outbreaks and increasing public concern over the safety of the food supply, irradiation was approved for use on poultry products. In 1999, irradiation was approved to curb pathogens in raw meats including ground beef, steaks, and pork chops. Irradiation is also used to preserve some meals eaten by astronauts during long-term space missions. Some consumer groups have raised concerns that irradiation might cause the formation of toxic compounds in food. Because of these and other concerns, only a limited amount of irradiated food has been sold in the United States.

Fermentation

Cheese Factory, Wisconsin Fermentation, a process in which micro-organisms convert complex organic molecules into simpler molecules, is used in the production of cheese. Bacteria convert sugars found in milk into lactic acid, a compound that prevents the growth of other, harmful micro-organisms and helps preserve the food. Read cheese-making operations.

Fermentation is a chemical reaction carried out by many types of micro-organisms to obtain energy. In fermentation, micro-organisms break down complex organic compounds into simpler substances.

Although chemical changes and microbial growth usually mean food spoilage, in some cases fermentation is desirable and micro-organisms are actually added to foods. For example, in the production of beer, wine, and other alcoholic beverages, yeasts convert sugar into ethyl alcohol and carbon dioxide. In the making of yogurt and cheese, bacteria convert lactose, a sugar found in milk, to lactic acid. Alcohol, acids, and other compounds produced in fermentation act as preservatives, inhibiting further microbial growth. In addition to its use with alcoholic beverages, cheese, and yogurt, fermentation is used to produce yeast bread, soy sauce, cucumber pickles, sauerkraut, and other products.

Pasteurization

Pasteurization involves heating foods to a certain temperature for a specific time to kill harmful micro-organisms. Milk, wine, beer, and fruit juices are all routinely pasteurized. Milk, for example, is usually heated to 63°C (145°F) for 30 minutes. Ultra-High Temperature (UHT) pasteurization, a relatively new technique, is used to sterilize foods for aseptic packaging. In UHT pasteurization, foods are heated to 138°C (280°F) for 2 to 4 seconds, allowing the food to retain more nutrients and better flavour.

Genetic Engineering

Genetic engineering is a means of improving the food supply even before harvest or slaughter by improving yields, increasing disease resistance, and enhancing the nutritional qualities of various foods. Broadly speaking, genetic engineering refers to any deliberate alteration of an organism's DNA. Genetic engineering has been practiced for thousands of years, ever since humans began selectively breeding plants and animals to create more nutritious, better tasting foods. In the past two decades, genetic engineering has become increasingly powerful, as scientific advances have enabled the direct alteration of genetic material. Genes have been cut and pasted from one species to another, yielding, for example, disease-resistant squash and rice, frost-resistant potatoes and strawberries, and tomatoes that ripen and therefore spoil more slowly.

Summary

- There are various services required by the farmer producers in the field of agricultural procurement and processing. Farmers are in need of agricultural inputs such as machineries, consumable inputs, post-harvest food product preservation facilities and storage services, standardization and grading, marketing information and market risk bearing.
- Supply cooperatives are a type of cooperatives specialized in supplying of agricultural inputs required by the farmer-members.
- Food Processing and Preservation is a branch of manufacturing that transforms raw animal, vegetable, or marine materials into tasty, nutritious, and safe food products. The modern food processing and preservation industry was born in 1809, when French chef and inventor Nicolas Appert, searching for a better way to provide food for Napoleon's army, devised a method for sterilizing food in tightly sealed glass bottles.
- There are various agro-based industries using food grains as raw materials. Fruits and vegetables are also used as raw materials. Dairy products and commercial crops like sugarcane, cotton, tea and coffee are also used by processing industries.
- Grain processing is about the most important activity from the final consumer's stand point within the marketing chain of the crop. Grain, for human consumption, is usually milled into flour or meal.
- Food preservation refers specifically to the processing techniques that are used to keep food from spoiling. Spoilage is any change that makes food unfit for consumption, and includes chemical and physical changes, such as bruising and browning; infestation by insects or other pests; or growth of micro-organisms, such as bacteria, yeast, and molds.

- Food preservation techniques also help eliminate the moisture or temperature conditions that are favorable for the growth of micro-organisms. As they multiply and grow, micro-organisms are capable of causing food-borne illness. They also break down foods, producing unpleasant changes in taste, texture, and appearance-changes that we recognize as spoilage.

Self-Learning Activity

Try to answer the following questions on your own:

1. Discuss about the challenges for grain marketing system.
2. What is the significance of agro-based industries?
3. Give an account of preservation of commodities.
4. What is the need for fermentation of certain commodities?

7

Cooperatives and Agro-based Industries

SUGAR COOPERATIVES

Sugar is one of the essential commodities of the consumers. It is being consumed by variety of ways in rural areas and urban areas. In tropical countries, sugar is manufactured using sugarcane. But in cold countries and European countries, sugar is manufactured from sugar beat, a root crop. In several countries, farmers go for manufacturing country sugar by crushing sugarcane. The method adopted is very old and crude. Lot of wastages arise through this old method. Modern days saw the organization of sugar factories, which has become an organized sector. Sugar factories have been organized in private sector, public sector and cooperative sector.

Sugar cooperatives are one of the important processing cooperatives, which may be classified as industrial cooperatives also. Sugar cooperatives are very popular in countries like India, Indonesia, and in several European countries.

Advantages

1. Sugarcane is long period crop that takes a year for yield. It is a high-income commercial crop. Sugar cooperatives can assure a good income to the farmers. Compared to the food crops, sugarcane being a commercial crop can fetch high income to the farmers.
2. For small farmers sugar cooperative provide good bargaining power. Small farmers can produce limited quantity of sugarcane. They may not have facilities to transport sugarcane and market it profitably. A cooperative sugar factory can give good bargaining power to the small farmers.
3. Through sugar cooperatives value addition is given to the farmers. Conversion of sugarcane and sugar juice into sugar is a value addition. Sugar is used as raw material for many products like alcohol, chemicals, beverages, etc. Such uses give additional importance and price to the farmers.
4. Sugar cooperatives act as *growth centers* in a locality and they work for the overall development of the particular location. This is possible by means of providing new employment opportunities to the skilled and unskilled manpower around the location of the sugar cooperative. The new income generated by the farmers and the people around the factory can provide good spending power. The farmers also add additional purchasing power through the sugar cooperatives. New industries and allied industries may also come around the cooperative sugar factory. This process is called as growth center.
5. Sugar cooperatives provide employment opportunity and encourage by-product development like distillery units, paper units, etc. As noted earlier, cooperative sugar factory can employ skilled and unskilled manpower and can provide employment opportunity to the local population. By means of organizing distillery units and paper units, additional employment can also be created.

6. Sugar cooperatives are also working for the principle *"Concern for Community"*. This denotes that a cooperative should not stop serving the members alone. On the other hand, it has to serve the non-members and community through several ways. They provide facilities like educational, medical, agricultural extension, etc. They also provide public amenities like construction of roads, rural electrification, distribution of agricultural inputs, etc. to the farmers.
7. They meet the important consumption need of the country by providing sugar at a reasonable price to consumers. In controlling the price of sugar, cooperative sugar factories balance the activities of the private sector.
8. Cooperative sugar factories can contribute to the export earnings of the country by means of exporting surplus sugar to foreign countries. Thereby, they contribute to the nations' cause of earning foreign exchange.

Membership

Those farmers who are producing sugarcane can become the members of sugar cooperatives. They are expected to make initial contribution heavily to the formation of the factory. When an individual is admitted as a member of a cooperative sugar factory, they should come to an agreement with the factory to supply all the sugarcanes to the cooperative sugar factory. Many times, members divert the sugarcane for the private sugar factories. When evidence is produced, such members are removed from the membership of the cooperative sugar cooperative.

Capital

A sugar cooperative is in need of two types of capital:

1. Block Capital or Fixed Capital
2. Working Capital

Block Capital: Heavy block capital for a sugar cooperative is needed to purchase land, to purchase machineries, and to construct buildings. Members cannot contribute the block capital needs. On the other hand sugar cooperatives can borrow these heavy amounts from industrial banks, foreign banks, etc.

Working Capital: Working capital is needed to meet the current expenditures of the sugar cooperative. Members' contribution of share capital can be used for the working capital purpose. In certain cases, sugar cooperatives also lend money for the farmers for the purchase of improved sugarcane seeds, fertilizers, etc. The money is collected during the sale of the sugarcane to the factory.

Mode of Business

Sugar cooperatives come to an agreement with each member to supply sugarcane of certain hectares. The farmer has to inform the cooperative about the maturity period and the factory will order for sugarcane cutting. After receiving the sugarcane cutting order the farmer will arrange to cut the sugarcane on his own expense and ask for transport arrangement. In certain cases the farmers have to make their own transport arrangements. After the sugarcane delivery is made, the farmer will be paid the money as per the prevailing price fixed either by the government or by the market. When a farmer has borrowed loan, the loan amount will be deducted from the final settlement.

Management

Cooperative sugar factories are managed like any other cooperative organization. But the board should consist of people who have vast knowledge and experience in the field of agriculture and manufacturing. They should also have the knowledge of business to sell the sugar and sugar related products for a profitable price. They should also give leadership for ancillary production and expansion of the sugar cooperative.

Rural Entrepreneurs

One of the most important contributions of co-operative sugar factories has been that they are increasingly becoming focal points for development of agro-industrial complexes in the rural areas. The Sugar Enquiry Commission of India has observed: "the setting up of a co-operative sugar factory has acted as a nucleus for social and economic development of the area around it and has helped to develop a new class of rural entrepreneurs". Many of them have undertaken development of by-products industries like alcohol, pharmaceuticals and paper projects, and have became the nucleus of development of other co-operative development activities like poultry, piggeries, lift irrigation schemes, solvent extraction plants and many others.

Alongside the welfare of the grower-members, the co-operatives have shown a keen interest in the welfare of the workers and the community, etc., and have contributed largely to the coming into being of township with schools, colleges, polytechnics, hospitals, places of worship, centers for cultural and social activities, etc., in the sugar factory areas.

Sugar co-operatives have afforded a unique opportunity to the small sugarcane cultivator to take full benefits of large-scale management and organization. Wherever co-operative sugar factories have been successfully established, they have proved instruments of development. Being decentralized processing units of small cultivators, sugar cooperatives are serving as effective agencies in the diffusions of benefits of development plans in an even manner and helping in the fulfillment of the concept of socialist pattern of society. One of the most significant benefits of co-operative sugar factories has been the spirit of self-reliance generated amongst small growers.

Linking with Consumer Cooperatives

For the effective distribution of sugar and to help the common man, the sugar cooperatives must have a link with the consumer cooperatives. They can supply the sugar to the Regional Consumer Cooperative Federations or to the cooperative wholesale stores. These apex institutions can distribute the sugar through the primary consumer cooperatives and cooperative supermarkets. During certain seasons, shortage may arise in the supply of sugar. During such times, the consumer should be put to lot of difficulties and the private merchants exploit them charging higher prices. Consumer cooperatives can avoid shortage and price rise of sugar.

SCOPE FOR SUGAR COOPERATIVE IN ETHIOPIA

Ethiopia, being an agricultural country, has enormous scope for organizing cooperative sugar factories. One of the preconditions to organize cooperative sugar factories is to construct irrigation dams and provide assured irrigation facilities to the farmers. Because sugarcane is a crop, which needs irrigation throughout the year. Here below, find the discussion on the scope for organizing sugar cooperatives in Ethiopia.

1. The country has good fertile soil and climate for the cultivation of sugarcane. Black soil is the most suitable soil for the cultivation of sugarcane. The fertility of the soil in Ethiopia is very high compared to other African countries.
2. Good rainfall is a positive factor. In highland areas and in several parts of lowland areas, good rainfall takes place continuously for four or five months in Ethiopia. Sugarcane consumes lot of water and rainwater can be harvested and used for this crop.
3. At present, very few private sugar factories are manufacturing sugar in Ethiopia. They hike the price artificially during several times. The private sugar factories price mechanism can be balanced by the cooperative sugar factories, the example has been shown in India where the cooperative sugar factories produce 50 per cent of the nation's sugar production.
4. There is good demand for sugar within the country. The growth of population is steady in Ethiopia. With the growth of population and increase in income and

purchasing power of the population, the demand for sugar will be growing steadily. Further, using sugar as a raw material, many of the industries like chocolate industry, ice-cream industry, breweries, chemical industries, etc.

5. Employment opportunities - Ethiopia needs fast industrialization to reduce the pressure on agriculture. A section of the population depending on agriculture must be diverted to industrial occupations. Sugar cooperatives can offer employment opportunities directly and allied industries like breweries, paper industries, etc. can provide further employment opportunities.
6. An export opportunity for sugar is bright. During several times, Ethiopia used to import sugar from foreign countries. This trend can be changed by organizing number of cooperative sugar factories. Sugar has continued export market. With lower cost of production, the sugar that could be produced by cooperative sugar factories can be exported competitively.
7. Government support can also be expected for licensing, capital formation, etc. The present democratic government is very favourable to the cooperative movement in Ethiopia. The government will certainly help the farmers to promote cooperative sugar factories.
8. Foreign private capital or cooperative capital can be invited to meet the financial needs of sugar cooperatives in Ethiopia. These are the days of economic liberalization. Cooperative sugar factories can have tie up with foreign private investment. Another alternative is capital can be mobilized from the cooperatively advanced countries like Sweden, Denmark, Ireland, Germany, etc.

DAIRY COOPERATIVES

Milk is an important liquid food for all ages of human being. Milk contains large amounts of essential nutrients and has been rightly recognized as nature's single most complete food. Nutritionally, milk has been defined as "the most nearly perfect food". Milk is an outstanding source of calcium and phosphorus for bones and teeth and contains number of vitamins. Milk as a food serves the purpose of the development of human being for their growth, reproduction, supply of energy, maintenance, and appetite satisfaction.

Specific Features of Dairy Industry

1. *Milk as raw material.* Milk has become an important raw material for human consumption. Milk is basically a liquid consisting of 90 per cent of water, which means it is a bulky and heavy commodity. It is produced on a daily basis. As a consequence, milk requires efficient transport system. Milk can be kept for few days, which places a time limit on the period during which it must be used or processed. Milk is perishable in nature and subject to adulteration. The quality of raw material is highly dependent on farm management. So quality regulations are necessary.
2. *Socio-economic position of dairy farmers.* Vast majority of milk producers are small-scale producers and have a weak position on the market and their supply is very limited. It gives daily income to the farmers. It is a labour-intensive industry and provides employment opportunity not only to the farmers but also to transport and processing sector. So in the rural development dairy sector plays a major role.
3. *Cooperative dairying.* In milk production cooperative dairying play a major role. According to International Dairy Federation survey in 1984 in 21 countries, together account for 55 per cent of the world milk supply and cooperatives marketed 86 per cent of the total sales. In New Zealand and India, 90 per cent of milk is processed by dairy cooperatives.
4. *Milk is a vulnerable at the same time expensive raw material.* Milk is used for the production of wide range of milk products and it is called as white gold. Processing industry is necessary to increase the value addition for milk. Without processing industry, milk sector cannot survive.

5. *Nutritional considerations.* Nutritional value of milk is high and of particular value when it is included in the diet of children. Even for elderly people and patients, milk is an important nutritional food.

Today, several forces like technological changes, economic liberalization, and privatization have created greater influence on dairy industry.

Importance of Dairy Cooperatives

1. Dairy is a subsidiary occupation for farmers and has become a standard source of income for the farmers. A weekly income is provided by dairy to the farmers. In agriculture, a farmer cannot get continuous income.
2. Scattered milk producers are united under the fold of cooperatives and middlemen exploitation was avoided. This is quite relevant in the case of small farmers and agricultural labourers.
3. Dairy cooperatives have increased the quantity and quality of milk production. In many developed countries, like Denmark and Ireland, and in developing countries like India, we could find this. India became the major producer of milk in the world in 2002 only out of dairy cooperatives.
4. Scientific method of rearing dairy animals has increased productivity and yield per cow. Dairy cooperatives provide scientifically developed feeding, rearing, and health facilities.
5. Modern methods of cow protection have been popularized by dairy cooperatives. Up-to-date veterinary services have saved milk animals from traditional diseases.
6. The system of milk procurement and payment on weekend has increased the confidence of milk producers over the cooperatives.

7. Speedy transport system, chilling plants, byproduct manufacturing, etc. have given new thrust to the dairy cooperatives.
8. Urban population has been assured of continuous supply of milk by the dairy cooperatives. In many countries, regular supply of milk and milk products have been assured by the dairy cooperatives.
9. Dairying has become an important occupation for women and income from dairy has increased their status in the rural areas.
10. Dairy cooperatives have wiped out poverty, unemployment, and low level of living in many developing countries. In other countries, such model can be applied to remove poverty.

Factors Favouring Milk Production

The following factors favour increase of milk production in developing countries, especially countries depending on agriculture.

1. *Current demand:* In many of the developing countries, the supply of milk and milk products is inadequate to meet the requirements of the country. Consequently, dairy imports for a high proportion of milk and milk products consumed in these countries. So, there is greater need to increase local milk production.
2. *Increasing population:* The current growth rate of population of developing countries is higher than developed countries. So, the per capita consumption of milk is expected to increase in future.
3. *Need for dietary improvement:* To counter malnutrition, in developing countries milk consumption must be improved especially for children.
4. *Rising economic levels:* The income level of population in developing countries is increasing, which can afford the population to consume nutritious food especially milk.

5. *Rising level of education:* In addition to the increase in economic level, the educational level of the population in developing countries is also increasing. This favours the high consumption of milk.
6. *Production potential:* Production potential for milk production is also high in developing countries. These countries have been traditionally producing milk and through modern methods and with the help of dairy cooperatives milk production and milk products can be increased.

Development Systems for Modern Milk Producers

Modern milk producers, especially smallholders have to develop their dairy farming through the following systems:

1. *Feeding systems:* Improved feeding systems through crop residues, pastures, concentrates, and supplements.
2. *Breeding systems:* Local breeds crossed with improved breeds can improve the quality of dairy farming.
3. *Production system for fodder:* Specialist fodder producers, roadside harvesting, and communal management are needed.
4. *Stimulus for development:* Banking institutions, government organizations, aid organizations, and NGOs can participate in dairy development.
5. *Management:* Disease management, housing, feeding for production, animal health, all need special attention.
6. *Applicable Technologies:* Protein feeding, urea and alkaline straw treatments, and vaccination programmes are needed.
7. *Market:* Local market, export market, supply for factories, etc. must be taken care of.
8. *Processing:* Processing activities at village level, regional, and national level must be developed.

9. *Integration of dairy system:* Dairy farming must be integrated with other farming activities like mixed farming.
10. *Animal output:* Dried cow can be salvaged for meat.

METHODS OF OPERATION OF DAIRY COOPERATIVES

1. Procurement Operations

The most important dairy activity is procurement of milk from the scattered milk producers. This is considered to be a primary activity of the diary cooperatives. the importance of procurement management is as follows:

1. The annual activity of a dairy cooperative is decided on the basis of procurement management.
2. A well arranged procurement system ensures the farmers a steady income and make them to have standard dairy operations.
3. Procurement management is a factor that decides the distribution system. Number of outlets, channels of distribution, etc. are decided on the basis of procurement management.
4. The operation of chilling plants, byproduct units, etc. depend on the procurement operations.
5. Fuller capacity utilization of plant and machinery of various dairy units is decided upon efficient procurement operations.
6. An efficient procurement operation balances the operations of lean season and flush seasons.

2. Methods of Milk Procurement

A dairy cooperative has to select the potential area for milk production taking into consideration of land utilization pattern, animal husbandry activities, marketable surplus of milk, availability of infrastructural and transport facilities.

A collection center or unit is set up to procure raw milk from a village. Under ideal conditions, the milk potential area for a dairy cooperative can be a radius of 60 to 65 km. The distance to be covered is to be estimated according to climatic conditions, timing of milk collection, and mode of transport. It is essential to see that raw milk reaches the dairy plant at least by 10 a.m., before the atmospheric temperature goes high, especially in the summer seasons, failing which milk turns sour.

While collecting the milk, the milk collector must examine the colour and smell the milk before taking the sample. Sample should be collected from each producer in order to verify the quality of milk in terms of fat content and to check the possibility of adulteration. Milk of poor quality should be rejected and the producer must be warned.

3. Milk Collection Centers

Milk collection centers organized by dairy cooperatives in important center of its area of operation has the following advantages.

1. They reduce the distance over which the producer must transport his milk.
2. They provide channels of communication between the producer, plant officials, and the cooperatives.
3. They permit convenient distribution of farm inputs such as feeds and fertilizer to the producer.
4. They make it convenient for milk to be tested for quality and advice the producers on clean and good quality of milk.
5. They assure farmers of a market at a reasonable price and thus, give incentive for higher production.
6. They help in pooling small quantities of milk from number of farmers into large amount for easy to transport.
7. They provide necessary cooling facilities for milk and extend the life of milk.

4. Transport Management

Transport is the basic function to be undertaken by a dairy cooperative. The need to have sound transport system by dairy cooperatives arises due to the following reasons:

1. Milk is a perishable commodity and its life is shorter than vegetables. So, effective use of this material by customers depends on the speedy transport system.
2. The distance between the producer and the consumer is wider and the time available for the distribution of milk is short. Only an efficient transport system will ensure smooth supply of milk.
3. As milk has short life, its life is extended by chilling the milk. Routing milk supply through chilling plants needs efficient transport system.
4. Dairy shortages or surpluses can be managed by well organized transport system.
5. It ensures regular supply of milk to consumers and stabilizes the price of milk in the open market.

5. Management of Seasonal Fluctuations

Milk production in general has two seasons, viz, lean season and flush season. During winter season milk production would be higher. The dairy cooperatives have to balance the demand and supply position. During flush seasons, the surplus milk can be converted into condensed milk powder and byproducts. During lean season, such milk powder can be reconverted as milk and supplied to the consumers. A precondition for the management of seasonal fluctuation is the management of chilling plants and byproduct plants. A well organized transport system also plays the role here. These plants must be operated to their full capacity to avert loss. Maintenance of plants must also be given importance in the capacity utilization. The district-level milk cooperatives and regional level federations can play a major role in solving these problems.

6. Problems of Dairy Cooperatives

1. *Seasonal variations:* As milk is not having balanced demand-supply conditions, seasonal variations in production affect the demand-supply position and price level.
2. *Marketing problems:* Milk being a bulky item must be marketed with speed. Otherwise, it may get spoiled and the producer cannot get good price.
3. *Purity of milk:* Milk supplied to the cooperatives must be pure, clean, fresh, and disease-free. Otherwise, a small amount of milk can spoil the entire container.
4. *Disease control:* Milk animals are very often affected by diseases. If enough attention is not taken it may lead to many problems. So, permanent disease control arrangement must be arranged.
5. *Efficient transport system:* Many dairy cooperatives suffer from efficient transport system. Only efficient transport system can make the cooperative success.
6. *Byproducts:* To provide higher price for the producers, dairy cooperatives must engage in the byproduct manufacturing. For this purpose, the regional and national dairy federations must take initiative.
7. *Export Avenues:* Dairy products in developing countries have good export avenues and this opportunity must be exploited by the dairy cooperatives.

DAIRY COOPERATIVES IN ETHIOPIA

There are two types of dairy cooperatives organized in Ethiopia. One by the producer cooperatives and the other by the service cooperatives. There are about 98 producer and service dairy cooperatives in Ethiopia. Exclusive dairy cooperatives were not organized in Ethiopia. Dairy Development Enterprise (DDE), a government enterprise, was having 14 dairy state farms under its control. These dairy farms supplied milk to Addis Ababa city.

Dairy Economy of Ethiopia

Ethiopia is an agricultural country and has the largest cattle population in Africa comprising 26 million cattle, 24 million sheep, 17 million goats, 7 million equines, 1 million camels, and 52 million poultry (FAO, 1981). In 1984 there were about 8.33 million cows and heifers older than two years, of which 65 per cent were yielding milk. Milk production in Ethiopia grew by 1.7 per cent between 1965 and 1976 and by 1.1 per cent per year from 1976 to 1985. During 1981 milk produced in Ethiopia was 27 kg/person. But it dropped to 17 kg/person during 1985. But it is still higher than the sub-Saharan African average of 15.7 kg/person. By 1983 local cows produced 400 to 680 kg of milk per lactation period of less than 7 months.

Milk Production

Sour milk or yoghurt is produced in the traditional system by leaving the fresh milk to sour for few days. Soured milk keeps longer than raw milk, so this process is useful for storing milk during the days of Wednesday and Friday where Coptic Christians are forbidden to consume animal products. Sour milk not consumed at home is usually sold to neighbours.

Sour milk can also be churned to make butter. The byproduct buttermilk is rarely sold and it is fed to calves, consumed at home, or further processed. Ethiopian farmers prefer butter manufacturing and for this indigenous methods are followed.

Production Systems

Milk production system in Ethiopia is followed on the following pattern:

1. *Pastoralism:* Pastoralists are livestock owners who maintain natural grasslands in arid areas (lowlands) with their herds of camel, sheep, goat, and cattle. Pastoralists move from one place to another place searching for fresh grazing areas. Milk is the main source of food for pastoralists.

2. *Agro pastoralists:* They are the farmers who cultivate food crops for food and for sale. Their livestock are fed on grazing land and crop land after harvest. Livestock are used for draught, milk production, and savings.
3. *Mixed farming:* Food or cash crop cultivation is the main activity. The farm size will be very small ranging from one to five hectares. Livestock are kept for draught, milk, and meat.
4. *Intensive dairy farming:* These farmers do dairy farming intensively and cultivate fodder crops exclusively. The dairy animals are not used for draught but manure is used for growing fodder. Milk is a major source of farm income. Labour intensity is high in this system.
5. *Peri-urban milk production:* This system is developed around cities that have high demand for milk. Milk is traded directly to the consumers of the city and is the major source of income to the farmers.

Measures to Improve Milk Production

1. *Reduced mortality of stock:* Efforts must be taken to protect cattle against the major diseases such as East Coast fever and tick-borne diseases.
2. *Lower calving intervals:* These are necessary to increase the number of calves born and to reduce the period when cows are not producing milk.
3. *Improved calve rearing:* This is necessary to ensure that a greater proportion of pure-bred and cross-bred are born and reared to reduce mortality.
4. *Upgrading indigenous stock:* In the short run it will be beneficial to the farmers to improve the productivity of indigenous stock through cross-breeding and better management.
5. *Adequate levels of feeding:* Efforts should be taken to reduce dry season shortage of feed. Such crops as maize, sorghum, and elephant grass must be used as feeding stuff.

6. *Commercial dairying:* Commercial dairying through cooperatives with production and market orientation must be encouraged to make the dairy farming a successful venture.

Scope for Organizing Dairy Cooperatives in Ethiopia

The scope for organizing dairy cooperatives in Ethiopia is very high. The following factors favour the speedy organization of dairy cooperatives in Ethiopia.

1. The high cattle population and dairy animals favour an atmosphere for increased production of milk and milk products through dairy cooperatives.
2. The farmers are traditionally experienced in managing dairy farming and they can improve their conditions by organizing dairy cooperatives.
3. With the economy moving fast, the income of the population is increasing, which may result in higher consumption of milk.
4. Milk being an essential food for children, the scope is very high to increase milk production through dairy cooperatives.
5. Enormous scope is there to have an export market. By means of setting processing units by dairy cooperatives, milk products can be exported to other countries.
6. The atmosphere with the government is favourable for the organization of dairy cooperatives in Ethiopia.
7. International help through NGOs can be available to organize diary cooperatives and dairy industries.

FRUIT AND VEGETABLE PROCESSING COOPERATIVES

The cooperative processing of perishable products like fruit and vegetable involves considerably high risks than marketing and processing of other crops, especially if the marketing is not confined to daily sales on local markets that require delivery to distant markets. Societies taking up these activities need experienced and well-trained management and sound financial resources.

Peculiarities of Fruit and Vegetable Processing Cooperatives

Such cooperatives are rare and they are coming under processing cooperatives. The peculiarities of such cooperatives are as follows:

1. They deal with commodities, which are perishable in nature. The specialty of the fruit and vegetable-processing cooperatives is to deal with agricultural produces, mainly perishable in nature. The life of such commodities are shorter and within the short period they must be sold or converted into different form like fruit juices, jam, or canned food.
2. The supply of such raw material is seasonal in nature. Like other agricultural commodities, the supply of fruits and vegetables are seasonal in nature. When supply is higher than demand, the farmers will be affected by getting lower price. Such trend could be avoided by means of taking the surplus produces for processing activities.
3. Dependence on nature to produce these commodities is high. Fruits and vegetables are prone to whether conditions, rainfall, climatic conditions, etc. Even the pest attack is high for such commodities than for cereal crops.
4. Modern technology is needed for preserving, storing, and manufacturing - Without using modern technology, a processing unit cannot run successfully. Even by using intermediate or indigenous technology, storing and preserving can be undertaken, but they cannot be effective for large-scale operations. Technology is also needed for various stages of manufacturing activities and conversion processes.
5. A brand name is needed to sell the finished products - The private sector and multinationals are able to shine in

this sector the creation of brand name. So, cooperatives must also go for brand names. In America, brand name such as Sunkist for citrus, Land O Lake for dairy and poultry products, Welch for grape juices, and Diamond for walnuts are used. In India, Amul is a popular brand name for cooperative dairy products. In Denmark, Lurbrand is a trademark for cooperative dairy products. Through brand name, the cooperatives can compete with the private sector and they can capture internal market and export market.

6. A good marketing outlet is necessary to sell the products. So enough promotional measures should be undertaken. Fruits and vegetables are perishable items and as such they are handled mainly by the private traders. Private traders have good marketing network among themselves. So for the processing cooperatives to undertake such marketing network is a serious problem. For the promotional measures, huge money must be spent on advertisement. This cost must be borne by the cooperatives.

7. An export market is desirable for such cooperatives - Fruit and vegetable processing cooperatives should not depend only on local market. On the other hand, they must take efforts to export their products to foreign countries. As the products would be costlier in the home country for the ordinary citizens, export avenue can balance the business transaction of the processing cooperatives.

8. Heavy capital will be involved for organizing such cooperatives - Processing cooperatives like other industrial cooperatives are in need of huge amount of fixed capital or block capital. This capital cannot be mobilized from the members. On the other hand, they have to look after the industrial banks, cooperative banks, or commercial banks. Heavy capital is needed to purchase land and construct the buildings, capital is also needed to purchase technology, equipment, and machineries. As

wear and tear would be high in these industries, replacement of machineries and spare parts must be done at a reasonable periods. Otherwise, it may lead to stoppage of work and production.

9. The loyalty of the members and continuous supply of raw material are very much needed. The members of such cooperatives usually have the attitude of selling the poor quality produces to the cooperatives and the good quality produces in the open market for a higher price. This attitude must be changed and the members must continuously supply quality produces to the cooperatives.
10. Such cooperatives have to compete with well-organized private sector and MNCs. In the field of fruit and vegetable processing private sector and multinational corporation have strong hold. For quite a long time, they have vast experiences in this field and they have specialized in technology, production, marketing, and promotion. Many MNCs have widespread hold over specified products throughout the world. So, to compete them is a challenging task.
11. Capacity utilization - The processing cooperatives have to take care of the fuller utilization of the installed capacity. Continuous supply of quality raw materials is a precondition for such capacity utilization. Stoppage of work due to power shortage, transport difficulties, labour problems, etc must be avoided.

Risks Involved in Fruit and Vegetable Processing Cooperatives

1. The period available to transport or transform these materials without any spoilage is very short. Any delay in transport through traffic congestion, breakdowns, customs controls, etc. can result in damage to the produce.
2. Any attempt to extend the marketing period by cold storage, deep freezing, refrigerated transport, treatment with chemicals, etc. or to speed up the transport by using air transport requires high investments and expenditures

and can lead to a steep increase in marketing costs. The feasibility of taking such a step depends largely on the relationship between the increased cost and the additional revenue expected from the sale of the produce and on the possibility of reimbursing any excess cost by paying less to the producer.

3. The delicate nature of the produce, which makes handling and packaging a difficult task that requires great care, skilled staff, and special packing material. In transporting these products, strong packing material is needed. On the other hand, such packing material must be durable and should not add weight to the product. The character of most fruits and vegetables as luxury rather than basic food, which makes them more dependent on changes in the consumers' preference and their purchasing power.

Reducing the Risks

Above risks can be averted through the following measures:

1. If the buyer could take the transport risk or if the society has enough processing facilities, the risk could be avoided.
2. The members of fruit and vegetable cooperatives have the feeling that the processing cooperative is the dumping ground to sell the poor quality produces. On the other hand, they sell quality produces to the private traders in the open market. This attitude must be changed for the successful running of the processing cooperatives.
3. Latest technology or affordable technology must be applied to the processing cooperatives. This can ensure the fuller capacity utilization of the unit and could render affordable volume of business.
4. Processing cooperatives of this type needs lot of working capital and long-term capital. Working capital can be increased stage by stage from the members and taking a part of the profit to the working capital. But long-term capital can be arranged through industrial banks and commercial banks.

5. As the products of fruit and vegetable processing cooperatives have very good demand in export market, a tie up can be arranged with other countries' consumers cooperatives and marketing cooperatives. For example, the National Consumer Federation of Sweden (KF) imports lot of cooperative products. Likewise, the cooperative wholesale store of England can also help the import of the products of cooperatives.

The management and working of fruit and vegetable processing cooperatives are the same as other processing cooperatives. In Ethiopia there is enormous scope for the organization of such cooperatives.

Scope for Organizing Fruit and Vegetable Processing Cooperatives in Ethiopia

1. The soil and climatic conditions are very favourable for the cultivation of abundant fruits and vegetables in Ethiopia.
2. Surplus production arises during several times. During such times lot of fruits and vegetables are sold for a lower price by the farmers. Processing cooperatives can change the situation and can provide stable price to the farmers.
3. Majority of the farmers in Ethiopia are small farmers and many of them cultivate fruits and vegetables. A stable income can be given to them by the processing cooperatives.
4. Many African countries like South Africa and Kenya have organized processing cooperatives and export fruit juices, canned foods and processed vegetables to foreign countries. By organizing processing cooperatives, Ethiopian farmers can also export such commodities.
5. One of the preconditions needed to organize processing cooperatives is the construction of modern godowns and refrigerated system. Government can come forward to arrange these facilities to the fruit and vegetable processing cooperatives.

MEAT AND EGG-PROCESSING COOPERATIVES

Significance

One of the contributions of Danish cooperative movement is the organization of meat and egg processing cooperatives. After the successful venture of organizing dairy cooperatives, the Danish farmers ventured to start meat and egg processing cooperatives.

The diversion of wheat as cattle and poultry feed led to the prospects of developing meat and poultry industry. As Denmark is popular for single-purpose cooperatives, they have started meat processing cooperatives and egg processing cooperatives successfully. This experiment has been successfully followed by Irish farmers, NewZeland farmers, German farmers, Dutch farmers, etc. In South American countries, these processing cooperatives are very popular. The following are the significance of meat and egg processing cooperatives.

1. *Cattle development:* In many developing countries of Africa, South America and Asia, cattle population is very vast and there is scope for processing this wealth.
2. *Nutrition:* Egg is a nutritious food for all types of age group like milk. Intake of egg and egg products is increasing in all countries year after year.
3. *Byproducts:* Number of byproducts like skin, bones, leather, etc are derived from cattle. Specialized industries for these byproducts can be organized.
4. *Technology:* For the scientific development of cattle and poultry population, modern technology must be planned in the fields of breeding, feeding, and disease prevention.
5. *Disease:* Cattle and poultry are susceptible to diseases like runderpest, yellow fever, bird fever, etc. Recently, for the past few years poultry birds have been affected by bird fever in several countries. Consumption of meat or poultry, which are affected by diseases, will be harmful to human beings.

Advantages

Meat and egg processing cooperatives provide the following advantages to the members, to the community, and to the nation.

1. *Additional source of income:* Cattle and poultry wealth are additional source of income to the farmers. In several countries, where pastoralism is practiced, the main occupation of the population is rearing of cattle. Cattle provide the major income for such population.
2. *Use of locally available resources:* For feeding cattle and poultry, farmers use locally available resources like grazing lands, hay from harvested crops, wasted grain, etc. Such agricultural residues will otherwise go waste. Farmers need not spend any additional money for feeding.
3. *Natural manure:* Cow dung and poultry waste are the best natural manure, which can keep the soil fertility forever. Nowadays, due to shortage of natural manure, farmers go for application of chemical fertilizers, which are very harmful to the soil. Even big farmers, having large size of lands can supplement chemical fertilizers with natural manure.
4. *Industrialization:* Meat and egg processing cooperatives faster the speed of industrialization. They are organized as small and medium industries and in due course they expand fast. Allied industries using cattle bone (a raw material for fertilizer units) can also be organized.
5. *Employment opportunity:* In developing countries, cattle and poultry rearing provides very good employment opportunity to the farmers. Cooperative processing units also provide employment opportunities to the skilled and unskilled people in the local area.
6. *Export opportunities:* The products of meat and egg processing cooperatives have enormous export market. The Danish cooperatives have shown the world the value of such cooperatives in the field of export marketing.

7. *Revenue to the government:* Processing cooperatives in the field of meat and egg provide substantial income to the government by way of paying various types of taxes. They also fetch valuable foreign exchange needed for the country. For example, in Ethiopia, meat export and skin export fetches considerable foreign exchange to the country.
8. *Disease prevention:* Meat and egg processing cooperatives have appointed qualified veterinary doctors and provide veterinary services and disease prevention measures not only to members, but also to the non-members. They provide preventive medicines and injections to the cattle and poultry population. They monitor health of the cattle and forewarn the members about disease attack, disease prevention, and other precautions.
9. *Improved varieties:* Meat cooperatives introduce crossbred varieties through the measures like Artificial Insemination. They have established special laboratories to preserve the semen of improved and crossbred varieties.
10. *Environmental protection:* Meat processing is undertaken under strictly scientific environment. Governments are very particular about the environment that could be spoiled by such industries. In the case of poultry industry, bird flu has become a threat and precaution measures are taken by the processing cooperatives to prevent such eventualities.

Conditions Favourable for Organizing Meat and Egg Processing Cooperatives in Developing Countries

Meat processing and egg processing cooperatives are prevalent in developed European countries. Many of the South American countries have organized meat processing cooperatives. In Asia — India, China and Japan — egg-processing cooperatives are very popular. These processing cooperatives provide great employment opportunities for the farmers. Such cooperatives can be organized by group of farmers, like other processing cooperatives. But they have to follow certain precautions like disease control, environmental protection, etc. Following are certain favourable factors for organizing meat and egg processing cooperatives in developing countries including Ethiopia.

1. *Location:* The primary precondition for organizing meat and egg-processing cooperative is the location. The location of the cooperative must be away from congested cities. The area must have sizeable population of cattle and poultry. These conditions are quite suitable for developing countries.
2. *Sizeable cattle and poultry pollution:* Developing countries comprising Asia, Africa and South America have sizeable population of cattle and poultry. For example, Ethiopia has the largest cattle population in Africa. But no meat processing or egg processing cooperatives exists in this country. These activities are handled by private sector. So, such countries have great scope to organize the above processing cooperatives.
3. *Income to the farmers:* Processing cooperatives in the field of meat and egg can provide supplementary income to the farmers other than agricultural income. Agricultural income is not continuous to the farmers throughout the year. But farmers can earn continuous income throughout the year through cattle rearing and poultry development.
4. *Value addition:* Such cooperatives provide value addition to the products. Instead of selling the cattle, through processing cooperatives meat can be prepared, preserved, packed, and exported. Likewise, egg can be powdered or processed and can be exported. Such conversion is called as value addition and provides good income to the farmers.
5. *Export Avenue:* One of the preconditions for the success of the above cooperatives in developing countries is the creation of export market. Primary cooperatives cannot

undertake such export marketing. On the other hand, primary-processing cooperatives must organize National Federations and such national federations can look after the export business.

6. *Government concessions:* In developing countries, the governments must provide certain concessions in the fields of licensing, taxation, regulations, export subsidies, etc. to the processing cooperatives. Because these processing cooperatives are earning income to the population and government, forms part of export revenue, and encourage employment opportunities. Governments must also make arrangement to provide long-term financial assistance to these cooperatives.
7. *Technical expertise:* Meat and egg processing cooperatives have to follow latest technology in processing, preserving, packaging, marketing, etc. Such technology is costlier and they have to be imported from foreign countries. The processing cooperatives can have tie up with other countries' cooperatives and can fulfill the principle of cooperation among cooperatives.
8. *Expanding market:* When the population grows the food needs of the country will also increases. Meat and egg form major part of the nutritious food item of human beings. Processed meat and egg are costlier and the population of developing countries may not have the purchasing power to absorb such products. So, naturally, the processing cooperatives have to concentrate on the export market.
9. *Quality products:* Cooperatives are meant for providing quality materials. The members of these cooperatives must make it a point to supply quality products to these processing cooperatives. They should not supply second quality products to the cooperatives.
10. *Continuous supply:* Like agricultural commodities, shortage may arise in the supply of cattle and egg to the processing cooperatives. When supply is not continuous, work

stoppage will be there. To avoid such problems, the cooperatives must plan their activities properly.

11. *Skilled manpower:* Highly improved technology is adopted by such processing cooperatives. Hence, skilled manpower is necessary to run the processing cooperatives successfully and profitably. So, the processing cooperatives must pay high salary than the private sector.
12. *Training and development:* The members of the processing cooperatives and the leaders of the cooperatives must be given continuous training in rearing cattle and poultry. They must also be given training to run such complex processing cooperatives. Field visits to similar processing cooperatives within the country and exposure visits to other countries can be arranged regularly to the members and leaders.

Management

Management of meat and egg processing cooperatives are the same like other processing cooperatives. While admitting new members, such cooperatives must be careful that the members have enough cattle population and poultry unit. The disloyalty of the members in the form of supplying units when the price in the cooperative is high, and not supplying the produces when the price is low in the cooperative should be avoided.

The board of directors or the committee members be elected regularly once in three years. Compared to other cooperatives, the management must be vigilant and cautious in running their cooperatives. Committee meetings and general assembly meetings must be held regularly as per the bylaw provisions. While distributing the net profit, a percentage can be set forth for environmental control and pollution control. Because the future of such industries depends on their commitment to keep a clean environment to the society. In several countries, such processing cooperatives have been closed down due to resistance from the local population for their negligence to keep the environment clean.

Problems and Solutions

The meat and egg processing cooperatives face several problems, for which solutions are also given below:

1. *Competition:* Such processing cooperatives are facing competition from the private sector. Private sector in these industries has long-standing record of service. They have developed internal and external markets for a very long time. So, cooperatives have to face competition from them by means of improving their quality and loyalty of the members.
2. *Continuous supply:* Another problem faced by such processing cooperatives is the continuous supply of quality cattle and egg. Several times egg production is affected due to diseases like bird flu. So, the cooperatives must undertake all precautionary measures to control such diseases.
3. *Veterinary services:* Many of the processing cooperatives neglect the provision of veterinary services to their members. Because, this is a specialized service, which is very costly. But neglect of veterinary service will bring down the quality of the cattle and products. The processing cooperatives can approach the government department to locate the veterinary hospital nearer to the processing cooperatives or while organizing a new processing cooperative, it can be located nearer to a government veterinary hospital.
4. *Disease attack:* Very often, cattle and poultry are affected by contagious diseases, which spread very fast from one country to another country. Processing cooperatives cannot be spared by such diseases. So, universal effort with the help of governments, WHO, and similar agencies must be undertaken.
5. *Technology:* Many processing cooperatives are following outmoded technology, which result in the poor quality of finished products. So, the processing cooperatives must import technology from advanced countries' processing cooperatives.

6. *Machineries:* Processing cooperatives need latest machineries for processing meat and egg. When technology is changing, improved technology demands the installation of latest machineries. Machineries are costlier and the processing cooperatives must make necessary arrangements to replace old machineries.
7. *Capital:* Meat and egg processing cooperatives need huge capital for setting the factory, purchasing technology and machineries. Many cooperatives have not modernized their factories due to lack of capital. The government and the financial agencies must come forward to finance such processing cooperatives. As an inbuilt measure, the processing cooperatives can approach the cooperative banks or public sector banks for finance.

Summary

- Sugar cooperatives are one of the important processing cooperatives, which help the farmers to increase their income and welfare.
- Sugar cooperatives are facing number of problems and major problem is relating to finance and the supply of raw materials.
- There is enormous scope for organizing sugar cooperatives in Ethiopia. This industry has internal market and export market.
- Dairy cooperatives have their origin in Europe and they have been organized in developing countries also.
- Dairy as an occupation gives regular income to the farmers.
- Dairy cooperatives have become a boom to the milk producers and they have increased the income and bargaining power of the milk producers.
- In developing countries, there is growing demand for milk and dairy cooperatives can make the dairy operations successful.

- One of the important activities to be undertaken by the dairy cooperatives is the procurement of milk. Quickness is very important in procuring the milk and dairy cooperatives open milk collection centers in their area of operation.
- An efficient transport system is a precondition for the success of diary cooperatives.
- Dairy cooperatives are facing certain problems of seasonal variations, heavy investment for processing units, transport difficulties, and competition in export market.
- Fruit and vegetable processing cooperatives are special types of processing cooperatives.
- Compared to other cooperatives, fruit and vegetable processing cooperatives face number of risk. Because, they deal with perishable commodities and they have to compete with the private sector and multinational corporations.
- Meat and egg processing cooperatives provide enormous income scope for the farmers.
- Ethiopia, being the country having largest number of cattle population in Africa, has enormous export market through the meat and egg processing cooperatives.

Self-Learning Activity

Try to answer the following questions on your own:

1. What are the advantages of sugar cooperatives?
2. Discuss the importance of dairy cooperatives.
3. What are the special features of fruits and vegetable cooperatives?
4. What is the scope for organizing egg and meat cooperatives in Ethiopia?

8

Promoting Cooperatives in Agribusiness

LINKAGE OF COOPERATIVES WITH THE NATIONAL ECONOMY

Cooperatives in Ethiopia are organized mainly in the field of agriculture. Agricultural cooperatives in Ethiopia are mainly undertaking input marketing and output marketing. Their role in processing is very minimal. These cooperatives join the mainstream of the economy by means of developing and increasing agricultural production. The national economy of Ethiopia is facing food shortage and the cooperatives struggle hard to attain food self-sufficiency within a short period of time.

Cooperatives are an important element in agribusiness today. The cooperative enterprise has its origins in the 19th century (1844) and has become one of the most widespread forms of business/economic enterprise. Cooperatives exist in all countries of the world and operate under diverse political systems. They are organized primarily to serve their members. Cooperatives are business organizations owned and controlled by those who use them. Their basic purpose is to serve the needs of their members (protection against exploitation) rather than make a profit on their own. Their growth in agriculture has been encouraged by favorable government policies that are designed to help individual farmers help themselves.

In Ethiopia, even though the three-tier system of cooperative was adopted, there were only two tiers realized up until now. These are primary cooperatives and secondary cooperatives in the form of cooperative unions. The basic unit in cooperatives is the primary cooperative. A primary cooperative is one in which shareholders are individuals, usually each of them with equal share. In secondary cooperatives however the members are primary cooperatives. The secondary cooperatives can undertake functions, provide services and make representations, which would be beyond the capacity of all primary cooperatives. Secondary cooperatives are a form of vertical integration providing the opportunity for economies of scale, scope for development and improved administration and operations.

NEED FOR PROMOTING AND STRENGTHENING COOPERATIVES

In countries like Ethiopia where millions of farmers are engaged in subsistence agriculture on fragmented farm plots, cooperatives play a significant role not only in creating an improved marketing system and providing market information, but also in other agricultural development works. It would be no exaggeration that neither meaningful agricultural development nor an efficient agricultural marketing system can materialize in Ethiopia without having a visible breakthrough in the development of cooperatives.

The FDRE government has given special attention to Cooperatives in its marketing policy and agricultural and rural development policies and strategies. The FDRE economic policy is known as Agricultural Development-Led Industrialization (ADLI), i.e., it is agricultural development-based industrialization policy. In this policy and other many strategies the cooperatives has given a vital role to play in order to achieve the policy objectives of rural and agricultural development. This is because, in a country like Ethiopia where majority of population are engaged in agriculture, cooperatives could play a very important role in reducing the time required for trade transactions and in buying and selling goods and services and reducing marketing costs, thereby creating an efficient and competitive agricultural marketing.

The assumed decisive role of cooperatives in agricultural development in general and agricultural marketing system in particular is not without reason. It takes a lot of time for farmers to be both producers and merchants simultaneously. Direct transaction between producers and consumers is not practical for many good reasons. It is both costly and time-consuming for merchants to buy commodities from millions of farmers in small lots. If it were to be done this way, the time wasted and the costs incurred in such an intermediary trading chain would be very great indeed. If each buyer and seller also attempts to be a standard-setter and a supervisor, the marketing system will be cumbersome and costly. Hence, in countries like Ethiopia, a system whereby the farmer attempts to sell his/her products individually can never be efficient and cost-effective. Obviously, such a system cannot possibly be a foundation for accelerated and sustainable agricultural development.

Cooperatives, and unions of such cooperatives, can, in principle, provide a reliable solution to the problem. They can have facilities to collect and provide storage services to farmers. Buyers can buy the amount they want from one such cooperative or a union or from a few of them. Cooperative can also be involved in products standardization and grading. They can standardize and grade products they collect from members, pack them properly and supply them to the market. They can gain the confidence of market participants as it is very likely that they themselves and government will institute measures to deal with any cases of fraud. They can also give training to farmers on product standardization and grading. As they base the prices they offer to farmers not only on the quantity supplied but also on the quality. They will be instrumental in instilling the commercial culture of quality-based production.

If farmers attempt to buy their requirements of consumer goods and inputs from merchants individually, the time it takes and the costs involved in such an intermediary trading chain will be excessive. If, on the other hand, cooperatives assume this task and sell consumer goods, agricultural inputs and implements direct to farmers, the time needed and costs incurred will be reduced significantly.

Cooperatives can also serve as intermediaries for importers and producers of agricultural inputs and implements. For instance cooperatives:

- Can own and lease agricultural machineries, implements and equipments to farmers.
- Can increase rural savings.
- Act as medium to increase farmers access to credit.
- A means to improve loan recovery from small farmers.
- Create Business opportunity for the banks through expansion of rural savings, lending money and rendering other services and contribute to rural financing.

Cooperatives can also render vital services other than those related to agricultural marketing. They can be a vital source for increased rural savings, a medium to greatly increase farmers' access to credit, a means to improve loan recovery from small farmers, and a business opportunity for the banks through expansion of rural banking operation. Cooperatives can go as far as establishing their own banks, taking deposits from the rural population, lending money and rendering other financial services as well, thereby contributing to the strengthening of rural financing. For instance Cooperative Bank of Oromia (CBO) can be cited.

Cooperative unions also provide marketing credits with feasible rate of interest for very much convenient maturity date. Such credits are provided through the supply of agricultural inputs such as fertilizers on credit and the principal plus interest will be deducted from the sale price of members produce. Such an arrangements assured member farmers with both credit facilities and adequate supply of agricultural inputs.

Cooperatives can buy agricultural machinery, equipment and implements to lease to farmer who individually cannot access these technologies. In addition to providing collection and storage facilities for agricultural products, they can also set up small agro-processing industries where processed agricultural products with greater value-added may be produced. They can also establish various social institutions to provide different kinds of social services.

Cooperatives have a separate arrangement for selling the members' produces. These special arrangements are discussed as follows:

SELLING ARRANGEMENTS BETWEEN COOPERATIVES AND THEIR MEMBERS

The principal question in Cooperatives is the procedure to be used in selling members' produce. There are two alternative methods of selling arrangements between cooperatives and their members.

The alternative Purchasing Policies are:

- Outright purchase from members
- Sale-on-commission
- Sale after grading and pooling

Outright Purchase

In this case members are paid for their produce at prices fixed by cooperative, at the time of delivery and the cooperatives takes title to the produce. The cooperative then resale the produce at the most advantageous terms it can secure. Profits made on the transaction will be used first to meet the operating expenses, any surplus balance being used or distributed by decision of the general assembly. This approach requires the cooperative to have high level of funds available. Since in the case of seasonal crops, a lot of produce is being offered within the immediate post-harvest period, a serious adverse cash flow situation can arise. This can be alleviated by a two-stage payment system whereby members are paid part of the sale price at the time of delivery and the balance after the cooperative has resold the produce.

The main objective to outright purchase is that the cooperative carries all the post-harvest risk including: falloff in demand, price fluctuation, reduce of produce value due to downgrading, deterioration giving rise to loss of quality and so value, failure of transport arrangements, spoilage, fire and theft. Some of these can be covered by insurance but most cannot. Generally this method is only acceptable where the risks incurred are limited and can be reasonably well assessed. This risks being taken to account, outright purchase has the advantage of permitting the cooperative to add value to the crop and thereby add to the profits of its members.

There are three principal ways in which a cooperative might add value to the commodity:

1. Produce can be stored for sale at a later date when prices have improved.
2. Value can be added through primary processing of crops. Cotton ginning is a good example of relatively simple and inexpensive process, which is best done close to the fields. The value of baled ginned cotton is normally considerably more than the sum of the value of raw cotton plus the cost of ginning.
3. Opportunity for adding value exists in the packing and presentation of the crop or in the case of livestock improvement in condition or quality before sale.

Sale-on-Commission

This is a far simpler; virtually risk-free operation, which leaves the cooperatives as the producers' agent with no legal title to the goods. All attendant risks therefore remain with the individual producers. The cooperative collects produce from member and sells in the most advantageous markets. It then deducts a commission at previously agreed rate from the sale price. The cooperative meets the cost of its expenses from its commission income. With the sale on commission system the cooperative avoids the need to finance crop buying and it minimizes its risks. In addition, much simpler producers are required and expenditure can be more accurately matched to anticipated income.

The main disadvantages of sale-on-commission is that neither the member nor the cooperative is able to exploit possible price improvement. Another is the possible delays in the producer receiving cash for his crop. No payment will be made by a cooperative, until it has been paid by customer.

Sale after Grading and Pooling

Cooperatives play two important and basic roles; these are: to set competitive pace and to act as power balancers. Frequently, the developing countries rural areas offered few alternative sources for essential farm supplies. In many cases farmers were afforded woefully inadequate service, yet were forced to pay high prices. By organizing a cooperative, farmers gained both their own source of supplies and a place to market their products; one that they owned, controlled and operated to serve their own interests. This alternative can serve to balance the power between farmer members and private enterprises. Since the primary objective of a cooperative organization is to benefit the needs of its farmer members, cooperatives often set the pace for new products and market services. As a result they are considered to be pace-setters.

Cooperatives are a means to guarantee quality products. Quality is defined as 'fitness for purpose'. Cooperatives are well known in supplying quality or "purest", full weight and measure of the products. Exact quantity and purest (quality) are part and parcel of the governing cooperative principles and values. The quality and quantity issues in cooperatives were well stated under the P (2) and (3) of the original nine Rochdale principles. These are:

(2) "That only the purest provisions of procurable should be supplied to members.

(3) "That full weight and measure should be given".

These principles were given to eliminate the act of adulteration and exploitation of customers through faulty weights and measures. Therefore as the acts of adulteration and cheating in weights and measures are against the principles of cooperatives and as they are expected to provide quality and full weight and measures, cooperatives generally deserve good public image and confidence of market participants. As a result cooperatives are a means to assure quality products and services at a reasonable price.

QUALITY IN COOPERATIVES

In past quality was monitored through applying prescribed maturity, grade and defect standards. More recently, the independent judgment system by government has been or is being replaced by organization self-regulation system. Therefore in quality control end-product testing is conducted, as a set of activities, which ensure that the end-product meets, required specifications.

Now a days Cooperative Unions are introducing the principle of Total quality management (TQM) in which the principles and practices of quality management are extended beyond the process line to all other activities. Such as supply, production, assembly, transportation, storage, processing etc. In general quality and cooperatives are inseparable.

For instance, Dairy Cooperatives and Unions are expected to conduct a regular raw milk test on fresh milk obtained from farmers. There are three essential raw milk tests conducted regularly during fresh milk procurement and assembly:

(a) *Organoleptic test:* Here the sense of smell is used to detect sour odors and perhaps tested too. Visual inspection reveals the presence of foreign matter.

(b) *Lactometer reading:* This test is conducted to detect any adulteration of the milk like the adding of water or skimming of fat

(c) *Butterfat test:* Fat content is the principal criteria used in deciding the level of payment to individual farmers. Raw milk is expected to have a fat content of at least 3.25 per cent.

Therefore, by conducting such tests cooperatives can ensure quality and strive to eliminate the act of adulteration and other unethical practices in their operations. These help the cooperatives to fast build good public image and as a result they deserve an optimum confidence from the general public as well as the market participants.

Hence, setting up and strengthening cooperatives is critical to agricultural development in Ethiopia. It is, therefore, necessary to identify the various problems which cooperatives in Ethiopia have encountered and to come up with acceptable solutions, bearing in mind that unfavorable experiences of the past should not be repeated.

PROBLEMS OF ETHIOPIAN COOPERATIVES

Cooperatives will not be able to play the role they should unless these basic problems are properly addressed. It is hoped that the increasing education coverage and tailor-made training will prepare better both cooperative leaders and members to meet their respective roles more effectively. Members will be empowered to exercise control on their leaders. This alone will not suffice to attain the desired level of administrative efficiency unless cooperatives can hire professionals and experts. Since the availability of such experts is wanting. Government should play its role to increase the supply. The Cooperatives on their part should create the capacity and show interest to hire such professionals. In order to strengthen the financial, audit and control system of cooperatives, Government should provide the required legal framework and prepare model directives and guidelines. In fact, an institutional network which provides technical and audit assistance and services to cooperatives at all levels should be put in place and progressively strengthened.

At present cooperatives in most places are financially weak and incapable of providing the services expected of them. They do not have the capacities to provide storage and transport facilities; not are they in any position to collect and sell farmers' products, nor supply agricultural inputs. Government support will continue to be necessary until cooperatives are reorganized and become financially strong.

Thus, assistance may take the form of encouraging public participation or provision of technical services. A system should be created whereby cooperatives can serve as agents of farmers in the distribution of agricultural inputs and, by doing so, strengthen their financial position. In order to strengthen cooperatives in terms of finance and administrative efficiency, they should be encouraged to organize into unions after they themselves have been individually and internally re-organized. It will also be necessary to create favorable conditions for them to borrow loans from banks as their financial positions and marketing structure improve over time. These measures will help improve the agricultural marketing system and expand other agricultural development services.

N.B. Part of this note was taken from the FDRE Rural development policies and strategies and methods published in November 1994 E/C. Therefore, you have to note that some of these problems were currently solved though some still persists. Therefore you are requested to identify the current problems of Ethio*pian cooperatives alone.*

EXPORT POTENTIAL OF AGRO-BASED INDUSTRIES

Factors that decide the export of commodities

In agriculture-oriented countries, export should be based on agricultural commodities or commodities processed using agricultural products as raw material. Ethiopia, being an agricultural country, has to depend on agricultural commodities and livestock for its export. Apart from this there are several factors that decide the volume of exports a country.

Surplus production

Particular agricultural commodity must be produced in large quantities and surplus must be available. Today, due to increase in population there heavy demand for food grains in foreign countries. Without having surplus production, if exports are resorted it may lead to price hike within the country.

Demand for value-added goods

There should be sufficient demand for value added commodities. For example, instead of raw wheat, wheat flour can have good need or demand.

Competition

No export takes place without competition from other countries. So our farmers must produce agricultural commodities at a lower cost that other countries farmers.

Price advantage

The commodities produced in our country must have less price in a foreign market, then only our products will have good demand in foreign markets. This is decided by the cost of production in side the country.

Government policies

Government policies in our country must allow the export of agricultural commodities. During the times of shortage of production our government may not allow export of food grains.

Currency restrictions and trade barriers

If there is currency restrictions in the exportable country, it may affect our exports. Many countries have introduced trade restrictions on the import of agricultural goods, as their agriculture and farmers may be affected. Under such situations our export may be affected.

Agro-based industries produce finished and semi-finished commodities, which are exportable in nature, if such commodities are surplus in nature. If the local or country' needs are satisfied, and if surplus is created, such commodities can be exported. The export potential of agro-industries are discussed as follows:

Tea and Coffee

These commodities are grown in countries like Ethiopia . Ethiopia is famous for coffee production and Ethiopian coffee is exported to several countries. Certain cooperative unions like Sidama cooperative union and Oromiya cooperative unions take the lead in exporting coffee beans. But the major problem is that the export is in the form of raw coffee beans and not in the processed form of powered coffee. By this act, only foreign companies are benefited a lot. It is time for the cooperative unions and other private companies to go for powering the coffee and export it through having some brand name.

Floriculture Export

This is one of the recent export oriented agro-based industries, that is flourishing in Ethiopia. To date more than 200 such units are organised by expatriates and Ethiopians. Such units are located in and around the capital city Addis Ababa. This city has certain advantages to the exporters. The international airport is accessible to the exporters within a hour or so. The surrounding locations have very good road and communication facilities. International banking facilities and similar facilities needed for the exporters are available in Addis Ababa city. As all the government offices are nearby, exporters difficulties are minimized. These floriculture industries provide employment opportunities to local population also. But they exploit the workers by means of paying very low wages. This situation must be rectified.

Food Processing Units

Food processing units have enormous scope of export potential in Ethiopia. Canned fruits, canned fish, processed meat and vegetables have good export potential in Ethiopia. The government must give incentives for such exporters in the form of providing tax holidays. Special industrial zones must be demarcated for such food processing industries. The government must also identify the suitable food products for export market by conducting market surveys.

Leather Industry

Ethiopia has the largest cattle population in Africa and it is one of the major exporters of hide and skin. Next to coffee, the major export of Ethiopia is leather products. But the major drawback of such export is that the country exports only the raw cattle skin instead of finished leather goods like shoes, bags, etc. If such industries are organized in Ethiopia itself large number of people can get employment opportunity. Ancillary industries could also be established.

Handicrafts Goods

Ethiopia is famous for its handicrafts, which are traditionally manufactured in this country for centuries. Such industries have lot of export potential and this should be exploited by the country. The initiative must come from the government side in the form of forming an export corporation exclusively for handicrafts goods. Through this process, the traditional industries get revival and the village artisans can get benefited by way of continued income and continued employment.

Teff Powder

Teff and teff powder have reasonable export market, but the problem is lack of surplus production. Good number of

Ethiopians are living in USA and other European countries and they need this foodgrain. If steps are taken to produce more teff, it can earn substantial foreign exchange to the country.

BUSINESS ESTABLISHMENT/FORMS OF BUSINESS ORGANIZATION

There are various forms of business establishments, namely sole enterprise, partnership firms, joint stock companies, cooperatives, and public sector organizations.

Sole Enterprise

Under the sole enterprise only one individual will form the company. Entire capital is mobilized by him. He is responsible for the decision-making and he is also responsible for the profit and loss of the unit. In sole enterprise, the liability is unlimited.

Advantages

1. Less capital is required.
2. The organization and management would be simple.
3. Decision-making is centralized and very fast.
4. He works hard to earn profit.
5. Less formalities are found in sole enterprise.
6. Such ventures are suited for small ventures like shops, trading, etc.
7. There is good scope for expansion.

Disadvantages

1. The liability is unlimited, if loss arises the unit has to be closed.
2. Proper accounts may not maintained under this system.
3. Due to unlimited liability, the entrepreneur must be very careful.
4. The future is not certain, if loss comes, he has to close it.

Partnership Firms

Partnership firms are organized by more than 2 people and it goes up to 20. There should be mutual trust, equal contribution of capital and openness in accounts, if a partnership has to succeed.

Advantages

1. Pooling of capital would be easier.
2. Variety of talents are mixed.
3. The burden of the organization is distributed.
4. Mutual watching of the progress, accounts, etc possible.

Disadvantages

1. Management would be difficult. Different opinions may come.
2. Indifference of one partner may spoil everything.
3. If success comes, partners may organisation, if failure comes, people will blame each other.

Joint Stock Company

Joint stock companies are organized as per the relevant acts of a company. They are registered firms and they have to follow the regulations of the country. There are two types of joint stock companies, namely, private limited companies and public limited companies. Under private limited company, the shares are mobilized among the shareholders and not allowed for the public. On the other hand, in public limited companies, shares are allowed for the public also. Very big companies and multi-nationals go for public limited company formations.

Features

1. It has legal entity.
2. The liability is limited.
3. There is continuity in the succession of shareholders. Shares can be transferred.

4. Ownership and management are separated. Through election, directors are elected.
5. There is accountability in running the firm. The board is empowered to take decisions.

Advantages

1. Joint stock companies can mobilize resources from various sources.
2. Shares are easily transferable and shareholder gets dividend every year.
3. Professional management is undertaken and there will be quality in service.
4. Loss or profit will be shared equitably among the shareholders.

Disadvantages

1. A man having more number of shares enjoys power and profit.
2. Lot of formalities and procedures are involved in running the unit.
3. Executives and employees may come and go. In that process, the trade secrets and the company secrets may be passed on to the rivals.

Cooperatives

Cooperation is a form of organization, wherein persons voluntarily associate for the economic interest of all other members. Cooperative venture is a joint venture and such organizations are organized under separate legal system.

The first successful cooperative movement in the world was started in England in 1844 by Rochdale Pioneers (28 people). Cooperatives are organized in agricultural and non-agricultural fields and the popular cooperatives are cooperative credit and banking, marketing cooperatives, processing cooperatives, consumer cooperatives, dairy cooperatives, housing cooperatives, etc.

Features

1. It is a joint venture.
2. Like-minded people join together.
3. Equality and democracy are preached – "Each for all, all for each"
4. One-man-one-vote principle is followed.
5. Honorary service is encouraged.
6. Unity in diversity.

Advantages

1. Exploitation is averted by cooperatives.
2. It is a joint venture and all resources are pooled.
3. Middle men are avoided, members are benefited.
4. Cooperatives provide income generation and employment opportunity.
5. Farmers, labourers, workers, etc are benefited.
6. Democratic management – Equal rights and participation in management.

Limitations

1. Cooperatives starve for resources.
2. Involvement of all the members are needed to run it successfully.
3. A strong leadership is necessary to make a cooperative successful.
4. Dormancy is a great problem in cooperatives.
5. In developing countries, government interference is very high.

Public Sector Organizations

Public sector organizations are organized by government. Some government owned corporations have indirect control by the government.

Merits

1. Public sectors organizations, with huge investment create employment.
2. There is possibility of collaboration with foreign countries.
3. Imported technology and latest technology are used.
4. These industries are established in the fields of steel, cement, etc. which provide infrastructure for the country.
5. The profit earned goes to government and spent for the public.
6. Public sector organizations build welfare facilities like schools, hospitals, etc.
7. The, encourage small-scale industries and allied industries.

Limitations

1. Inefficiency and corruption are high.
2. Majority of the public sector organizations run on loss.
3. Workers are given freedom and production goes down.
4. Decisions are delayed, red-tapism enters.
5. Government interference will be high.

Common Characteristics of Cooperatives with other Business Sectors

1. Both cooperatives and non-cooperatives businesses engage in profit making activities. However, the relationship that they have with profit is different. Non-cooperatives are profit motive business. On the contrary cooperatives, even though in order to stay in the business making surplus, are not profit motive rather they are service motive.
2. Both cooperatives and non-cooperatives businesses sectors have legal personality, though some secret

businesses are there in the sector. However, the Ethiopian commercial code states that all business organizations should be registered by appropriate authority and obtain legal personality before starting any business. Cooperatives are not governed by commercial law, rather special resolution that suits the cooperatives principles, values and conditions should be enacted. That is why the FDRE government has enacted Cooperative Societies Establishment Proclamation No 147/1998, which is the existing proclamation of Ethiopian Cooperative Societies.

COOPERATIVES AND OTHER BUSINESS SECTORS – THE COMPARATIVE ANALYSIS

The Cooperative societies are established to attain one or more of the following objectives:

1. To solve problem collectively which members cannot individually achieve.
2. To achieve a better result by coordinating their knowledge, wealth and labour.
3. To promote self-reliance among members.
4. To collective protect, withstand and solve economic problems.
5. To improve the living standards of members by reducing production and service costs by providing input or service at a minimum cost or by finding a better price to their products or services.
6. To expand the mechanism by which technical knowledge could be put into practice.
7. To develop and promote savings and credit services.
8. To minimize and reduce the individual impact or risks and uncertainties.
9. To develop social and economic culture of members through education and training.

There are four fundamental concepts that differentiate a cooperative from other forms of business enterprise. These are:

1. Basic purpose

The first distinctive concept is that cooperatives are organized to help member/patrons increase the profits from their own business. Cooperatives achieve this goal by providing member/patrons with the products and services they need to lower their costs and/or to operate more efficiently. The total emphasis is on the member user, on the other hand, is to generate a profit for the owners of the business.

Often cooperatives and non cooperative businesses operate similarly in the same market-place, but there are many cases where their distinctively different purposes lead to distinctively different operating decisions. In general the orientation of the cooperatives toward meeting members' needs triggered a very different set of operating decisions from those of the non-cooperatives.

2. Cooperatives operate at cost

Cooperatives are obligated by their laws (bylaws) under which they are incorporated to return to their members' income in excess of the expenses generated by number business in the form of dividend. This income is distributed to individual members in proportion to the volume of business that they have brought to the cooperative. The aforementioned obligation is the primary factor that separates cooperatives from other forms of business. Non-cooperatives are not to obliged and after paying tax any profits that may be due, will return to the owners of the business or will keep the profits in the business as retained earnings their future growth.

From a technical point of view cooperatives do not make profit, since they are obliged bylaw to return to their members all income that in non-cooperative enterprises would be viewed as profit. This is why cooperatives are sometimes called *non-profit organizations.* Actually even non-cooperatives are free to return their profits to their customers in proportion to the amount of business that the customers have transacted, just as cooperatives do. But since the basic purpose of non-cooperatives is to return profits to their investors, few choose this alternative.

Non-cooperatives are not so obligated and after paying tax any profits that may be due, will return profits to the owners of the business in proportion to the owners' investment, or will keep the profits in the business as retained earnings for future growth.

3. Member Controlled, Member Owned

A fundamental and unique principle under-girding cooperatives is that must be owned and controlled by the people who conduct business with them. It is imperative that cooperatives maintain their orientation toward servicing those who patronize them. And there is no better way to ensure this than to require that the cooperative be controlled by active member patrons who are also owners of the business.

Non-cooperatives, however, place total control in the hands of owner-investors and base the degree of control accorded to each owner-investor exclusively on the amount that the owner has invested in the business. It makes no difference the owners even patronize the business. In fact, in non-cooperatives the owner may never see the business or take any role in decision-making. This is particularly true in larger corporations.

Member control of cooperative is executed through boards of directors, which are elected in open-elections from the ranks of active membership based on one-man one-vote principle. The board shoulders the responsibilities of sensing and representing the best interest of all members, setting overall policy, making important management decisions, hiring and directing top management, and monitoring the cooperative performance in achieving its objectives. However some highly critical decisions involving such issues as mergers or large investments may be taken directly to the membership for vote.

In a non-cooperatives business, on the other hand, the directors are elected by owners, whose number of votes is determined individually by the amount of stock they own. Consequently most board members are stockholders with relatively large ownership interests.

4. Limited Returns on Capital

Since the basic purpose of cooperatives is to operate at cost in order to benefit member/patrons directly in their own business. Limiting returns on member equity to a nominal amount, not greater than the going interest rate, simply ensures that members holding stock in the cooperative are not tempted to view the cooperative as an investment in and of itself, but rather as a service to their own business.

In fact most cooperatives pay no dividends on their stock; therefore limiting returns is merely an academic point. But it is important to recognize the limited-returns principle, since it ensures that the purpose of the cooperative – to help farmers help themselves rather than to become an investment company – is realized.

Summary

- Cooperatives are engaged in procuring and selling the commodities of the farmers at a price higher than the market price. This makes the cooperatives as popular business organizations.
- Cooperatives follow various methods of selling the produces of the farmers. This makes the farmers to take advantage of various methods, which have merits and disadvantages at equal footing.
- The export of agricultural commodities in a country is decided by several factors like surplus production,

competition in the foreign market, commercial policies of the importing country, etc.

- The popular agricultural commodities that have a place in Ethiopia's export avenue are coffee, leather goods and handicraft goods.
- Cooperatives have to compete with other forms of business organizations like, sole enterprise, partnership firms, joint stock companies, etc.
- Cooperatives and other non-cooperative business enterprises are all operating in the same market, with different operational decisions. Even though cooperatives engage in profit making business activities, profit is not their main objective as it is organized to provide services to members. Cooperatives achieve this goal by providing member patrons with the products and services they need to lower their costs and/or to operate more efficiently. Therefore cooperatives are not for profit but service organizations.
- Cooperatives are organized and controlled by member users. However in non-cooperatives, the business is controlled by non-member professional managers. Member control of cooperative is executed through boards of directors, which are elected in open-elections from the ranks of active membership based on one-man one-vote principle.
- Cooperatives are obligated by their laws (bylaws) under which they are incorporated to return to their members' income in excess of the expenses generated by number business in the form of dividend. This obligation is the primary factor that separates cooperatives from other forms of business. Non-cooperatives are not to oblige and after paying tax any profits that may be due, will return to the owners of the business or will keep the profits in the business as retained earnings their future growth.

- Since the basic purpose of cooperatives is to operate at cost in order to benefit member/patrons directly in their own business. Limiting returns on member equity to a nominal amount, not greater than the going interest rate, simply ensures that members holding stock in the cooperative are not tempted to view the cooperative as an investment in and of itself but rather as a service to their own business.

Self-Learning Activity

Try to answer the following questions on your own:

1. What is outright purchase system?
2. What are the actors who decide the export of commodities?
3. How do cooperatives operate at cost?
4. What are the limitations of cooperatives in agribusiness?

Glossary

Agro-industry: Set of manufacturing activities which preserve and process raw materials from agriculture, forestry and fisheries.

Break-even point: The level of production at which all costs are covered.

Cash flow: The record of monies received and paid by the company.

Certificate of origin: This is usually handled by a shipping agent and standardized forms are used.

Commercial invoice: Sales document which includes standard information (date of issue, name and address of buyer and seller, contact number, description of goods, unit price, number of units, packages, total weight, terms of delivery and payment).

Competitor: Another business selling similar types of products to the same target customers.

Consumer: The person or household who is the final buyer of a product.

Creditors: People who are owed money by a business.

Customer: A person, firm or institution who buys a product.

Collective action: Initiative of a group motivated by a shared goal to achieve a common or group interest.

Comparative advantage: Comparative agrifood advantage is derived basically from a country's natural assets, characterized mainly by a wide diversity of ecosystems, climates, species and the availability of water resources, as well as by geographical situation, exchange rates, and other factors.

Competitive advantage: A company has competitive advantage when it is in a better position than its rivals to secure customers and defend itself against competitive forces. Some sources of competitive advantage are: making better-quality products; providing better customer service; achieving lower costs than rivals, or designing a product with a better return than rival brands.

Competitiveness: The ability to place the goods one produces on the market, under conditions of fair competition, in such a way as to improve people's welfare.

Debtors: People who owe money to a business.

Demand: The amount of goods that customers want or need to buy.

Depreciation: Decrease of value of capital equipment due to wear and tear and the passage of time.

Efficiency: A measure of the amount of production from a certain level of inputs.

Equity finance: Money put into a business by the owner.

Export permits: From the Government of an exporter.

Feasibility study: Systematic investigation of an idea for a new product or process to see if it can work, i.e. to see if it is feasible.

Fixed costs: Costs of production that do not vary with the amount of goods produced.

Inventory: Amount of inputs, unfinished and finished products at a given time.

Investment: Putting money, fixed and current assets into a business.

Invoice: A bill requesting payment.

Market size: The total amount of a product that is bought per month or per year in volume or value terms.

Marketing: The series of activities to identify customers and then satisfying their needs by providing them with the products they want.

Order: A written request for goods or services.

Profitability: Income minus expenses.

Proforma invoice: A delivered cost estimate usually required for a successful sale.

Production planning: Calculating and predicting the number and amount of inputs needed to make a product.

Productivity: Output per unit cost.

Promotion: A set of activities to raise awareness of a product and increase sales.

Receipt: A written acknowledgement of payment.

Revenue: Income derived from product sales and from other sources such as interest rents etc.

Servicing: Planned inspection and maintenance of equipment.

Staff development: Training and other means of increasing a person's effectiveness to do a job.

Stock: Materials waiting to be used or sold.

Variable costs: Costs of production that vary according to the amount of goods produced.

Yield: Weight of food after processing compared to weight before processing.

References

Abrahamsen, Martin, 1976, *Cooperative Business Enterprise*, New York, McGraw Hill.

Anastassopoulos G., & R. Rama (2005), "The Performance of Multinational Agribusinesses: Effects of Product and Geographical Dispersion", in *Multinational Agribusinesses*, ed. Ruth Rama, Food Products Press, New York.

Athukorala, Premachandra and Kunal Sen 1998, "Processed Food Exports from Developing Countries: Patterns and Determinants." *Food Policy* 23(1): 41.

Barlowe (1986), *Land Resource Economics*, Prentice Hall.

Batille-Chedotel, F. and Huntizinger, F., 2004, Faces of Governance of Production Co-operatives: An Exploratory Study of Ten French Cooperatives, *Annals of Public and Cooperative Economics*, 75/1: 89-111.

Bibby, A. and Shaw, L., 2005, *Making a Difference: Co-operative Solutions to Global Poverty*, Manchester: Co-operative College.

Birchall, J., 2004, *Co-operatives and the Millennium Development Goals* (Geneva: ILO).

Birchall, J., 2006, *Co-op: The People's Business*, Manchester: Co-operative College.

Birchall, J. and Simmons, R., 2004, "The Involvement of Members in the Governance of Large-Scale Co-operative and Mutual Businesses: A Formative Evaluation of the Co-operative Group", *Review of Social Economy*, 62/4: 487-515.

Birchall, Johnston, 1993, *Co-op: the People's Buiness*, Manchester: Manchester University Press.

Cramer Gail, 1993, *Grain marketing*, Westview Press.

Davis, P, 1995, "Co-operative Management and Co-operative Purpose: Values, Principles and Objectives for Co-operatives into the 21st Century", discussion papers in Management, No. 95/1, Management Centre, University of Leicester, January, 1995. p. 22.

Davis, P., 1999, *Managing the Co-operative Difference. A Survey of the Application of Modern Management Practices in the Co-operative Context*, Co-operative Branch, ILO, Geneva. p. 134. ISBN 92-2-111582-8.

Davis, P., 2004, *Human Resource Management in Co-operatives. Theory, Process, and Practice*, ILO Cooperative Branch, Geneva.

Downey, Trocke, 1981, *Agribusiness Management*, New York.

Duff Kenneth, 1979, *Principles of Management in Agribusiness*, Reston Publishing, Reston, USA.

FAO, 1997, "Guidelines for Small Scale Fruit and Vegetable Processors", by P.J. Fellows. FAO, *Agricultural Services Bulletin*, No. 127, Rome.

FAO, 2005, "Business Management for Small-scale Agro-processors". AGSF Working Document No. 7, Rome.

Fellows, P.J. & Axtell B., 2004, *Opportunities in Milling and Baking*. Wageningen, Netherlands, Technical Centre for Agricultural and Rural Co-operation.

Fellows, P.J. & Axtell, B., 2001, *Opportunities in Food Processing — Setting Up and Running a Small Food Business*. Wageningen, Netherlands, Technical Centre for Agricultural and Rural Co-operation.

Gibbon, Peter, 2003, "Commodities, Donors, Value-Chain Analysis and Upgrading," paper prepared for UNCTAD, Danish Institute for International Studies, Copenhagen.

Goldberg Ray, 1968, *Agribusiness Coordination*, Harvard Business School.

Goodwin John 1982, *Agricultural Economics*, Reston Publishing, Reston USA.

Helm F.C , 1968, *The Economics of Cooperative Enterprise*, University of London Press, London.

Jaffee, Steve, Ron Kopicki, Patrick Labaste and Iain Christie, 2003, "Modernising Africa as Agro-Food Systems: Analytical Framework and Implications form Operations." Africa Region Working Paper Series No. 44. World Bank, Washington, D.

Kadlec John, 1985, *Farm Management*, Printice Hall.

Kaplinsky, Raphael, 2005, *Globalization, Poverty and Inequality*, Cambridge: Polity Press.

Lele, U., 1989, "Markets, Marketing Boards and Coops in Africa", Discussion Paper No. 11, Washington DC, World Bank.

Maleorn Sargent, 1982, *Agricultural Cooperation*, Gower Publishers London.

Mickel Brown, 1995, *Rural Cooperatives in Africa, African's Choices*, Pengiun.

Mohanty, S.K., 2006, "Trade and Environment Dimensions in the Food and Food Processing Industries in Asia and the Pacific . " New Delhi, India.

Pekka Hussi, et.al., 1993, *The Development of Cooperatives and other Rural Organizations – Role of the World Bank*, World Bank.

Penson et al., 1986, *Introduction to Agricultural Economics*, Printice-Hall.

Provisional Military Government of Socialist Ethiopia, 1978, Proclamation to Provide for the Establishment of Cooperative Societies in Ethiopia, *Proclamation No. 138 of 1978*, Addis Ababa.

Provisional Military Government of Socialist Ethiopia, 1979, *Guidelines for Small Scale Industries and Artisans' Cooperatives of Ethiopia*, Addis Ababa.

Provisional Military Government of Socialist Ethiopia, (1979), *Guidelines for Farmers Cooperative Development in Ethiopia*, Addis Ababa.

Roy Edwell, 1994, *Economics: Applications to Agriculture and Agribusiness*, The Interstate Printers, Danville, USA.

Tegene Teka, *Coops and National Development: The Ethiopian Experience*, paper presented for the FAO Workshop on "The Transformation of Agrarian Systems in Centrally Planned Economies in Africa", Arussia, Tanzania, published by the Institute of Development Research, Addis Ababa University, IDR Working Paper No. 18, Aug. 1984.

Tegene, T. "Producers Coops and Rural Development in Ethiopia", paper presented at the Economic Commission for Africa (ECA), Addis Ababa, Oct 7-11, 1985.

Tweetten Luther, 1989, *Agricultural Policy Analysis*, WestView Press, USA.

Wills Walter, 1979, *An Introduction to Agribusiness Management*, Interstate Press, Danville, USA.

Wright, David H., 1979, *Co-operatives and Community*, London: Bedford Square Press.

Index

J

L

M

N

O

P

R